NO
ROOM
for
BULLiES

LESSON PLANS FOR GRADES 5-8

Also from the Boys Town Press

For Teachers

Teaching Social Skills to Youth
Tools for Teaching Social Skills in School
More Tools for Teaching Social Skills in School
No Room for Bullies
The Well-Managed Classroom
Teaching Social Skills to Youth with Mental Health Disorders
Effective Study Strategies for Every Classroom
Working with Aggressive Youth
The Worst Day of My Life Ever! Activity Guide for Teachers
I Just Don't Like the Sound of No! Activity Guide for Teachers
Sorry, I Forgot to Ask! Activity Guide for Teachers
Teamwork Isn't My Thing, and I Don't Like to Share! Activity Guide for Teachers
Adolescence and Other Temporary Mental Disorders (DVD)
The 100-Yard Classroom

For 5-8 Graders

Friend Me!
A Good Friend
Who's in the Mirror?
What's Right for Me?
Basic Social Skills for Youth

For K-6 Graders

(By Julia Cook)
The Worst Day of My Life Ever!
I Just Don't Like the Sound of No!
Sorry, I Forgot to Ask!
Teamwork Isn't My Thing, and I Don't Like to Share!
Making Friends Is an Art!
Cliques Just Don't Make Sense!
El Peor Dia de Toda Mi Vida

**For a Boys Town Press catalog, call 1-800-282-6657
or visit our website: boystownpress.org**

NO ROOM for BULLiES

LESSON PLANS FOR GRADES 5-8

Kim Yeutter-Brammer, M.B.A.
Susan Lamke
Jo C. Dillon
Matthew J. Minturn
Alesia K. Montgomery
Kristina Krause, M.A.

BOYS TOWN. Press

Boys Town, Nebraska

No Room for Bullies: Lesson Plans for Grades 5-8
Copyright © 2012 by Father Flanagan's Boys' Home
ISBN 978-1-934490-33-4

Published by Boys Town Press
14100 Crawford St.
Boys Town, Nebraska 68010

Boys Town Press is the publishing division of Boys Town, a national organization serving children and families.

Boys Town National Hotline
1-800-448-3000
A crisis, resource and referral number for kids and parents.

10 9 8 7 6 5 4 3 2 1

Table of Contents

INTRODUCTION 1

PART I: Understanding the Problem

UNIT 1 BULLYING DEFINITION

Lesson 1: Identifying Bullying. 6
Lesson 2: Fact or Fiction? 8

UNIT 2 KEY PLAYERS

Lesson 3: Bystanders 14
Lesson 4: Bullies. .22
Lesson 5: Bullies. .23
Lesson 6: Victims/Targets 25

UNIT 3 IMPACTS OF BULLYING

Lesson 7: Bystanders 32
Lesson 8: Bullies 33
Lesson 9: Victims/Targets 35

UNIT 4 AREAS WHERE BULLYING
TAKES PLACE

Lesson 10: Classroom 38
Lesson 11: Common Areas 40
Lesson 12: School Bus 41
Lesson 13: School Grounds. 43
Lesson 14: School Watch 45
Lesson 15: Cyberbullying 46
Lesson 16: Cyberbullying 49

UNIT 5 SPECIAL TOPICS

Lesson 17: Sexual Bullying 52
Lesson 18: Reporting Mechanism. 55
Lesson 19: Trends in Bullying. 56

PART II: Solving the Problem

UNIT 6   SOCIAL SKILLS FOR BULLIES

Lesson 20: Accepting Differences 58
Lesson 21: Expressing Empathy and
Understanding for Others 60
Lesson 22: Apologizing 65

UNIT 7   SOCIAL SKILLS FOR VICTIMS/TARGETS

Lesson 23: Making Friends 68
Lesson 24: Asking for Help 71
Lesson 25: Teasing vs. Bullying 73
Lesson 26: Responding to Bullying 78

UNIT 8   SOCIAL SKILLS FOR BYSTANDERS

Lesson 27: Resisting Negative Peer Pressure 84
Lesson 28: Reporting Others' Behavior 87
Lesson 29: Showing Concern for Someone
Who's Been Hurt 89

UNIT 9   PROBLEM SOLVING

Lesson 30: POP – Problem, Options, Plan 92
Lesson 31: Problem Solving with SODAS 95
Lesson 32: Class Meetings 99
Lesson 33: Reporting Guidelines 101

PART III: Appendix

Tips for Teachers 106
Tips for Administrators 107
Tips for Teachers Working with Parents 108
Anti-Bullying Social Skills 109

Introduction

The following are actual phone calls and emails from young people to the Boys Town National Hotline^SM.

- Nathan -

"I am a fifteen-year-old guy in ninth grade. There is a girl in my class who thinks she can bully me and put me down. It hurts my feelings. She kicks my chair. She is aware that I don't like to talk in school and that I don't stand up for myself. If I say something to her, she would just say, "Who are you talking to?" I can stand up to a guy, but this is a girl! She is controlling me and putting me down constantly; it makes me look like a freak-loser. All the other kids in the class are seeing what she is doing to me. If I stand up to her, I just know that the other kids in the class would be DYING to say something mean to me. Then I will have to stand up to all of them and that is too much! No one likes me; I am just a pushover. Help me."

- Paige -

"My sister and I have been getting bullied by a boy named Nick. In the past, he has come up to us and cussed us out. He was just playing though. After a while, it got really annoying. He always called us "bitches" and "motherf......s." Today his friend Andre chatted with my sister on Facebook and started calling her a "bitch" and insulting her. A few minutes later, Nick started doing the same thing. I talked to Nick and told him I would see him and Andre in the Dean's of-

fice Monday. Nick got scared and posted an apology on my wall. But, Nick and Andre were posting on other peoples' walls things like, "OMG...I'm gonna get suspended coz of Paige and Sabrina." Now everyone is getting involved. I am still going to go to the Dean's office on Monday because my mom told me to. I am just really scared that if they do get suspended, the whole school will hate me! HELP!"

- Emily -

"Hi, I am fourteen years old and a new student in my school. I have been bullied to my breaking point. I have nobody here. I am alone and no one understands me. They call me names every day like "whore" and "slut." Because of that, a boy I was dating broke up with me and called me names. They make me want to crawl into a hole and die. I have tried my whole life not to feel this way. I have been broken for the last time. I feel like I want to go back to cutting myself. I have only one person – my best friend. I feel so depressed. There is no escape. Everywhere I go their voices pierce my ears like a bullet from a gun. As the whole school bullies me, it drives me to the edge. Life isn't fun anymore. It's like not even worth living. If my school knew what it was like for people to deal with this every day, they could see that walking the halls is like my own personal hell. When I go home, hell comes with me. I get bullied over the Internet as well. No one understands me, and nobody ever will. What should I do?"

♪ ♬ ♩

Nathan, Paige, and Emily are not alone. Research shows that bullying is a far-reaching, all-too-common occurrence among young people. And it can take place just about anywhere. For example, in a recent survey of fourth through eighth graders, forty-two percent reported having been bullied online.[1] The same survey found that fifty-eight percent of kids admit that mean, hurtful things have been said to them online.

Bullying also can happen face to face, and it can be directed toward many things, including one's gender, sexual orientation, or physical characteristics. In 2011, the National Education Association (NEA) reported that twenty-three percent of bullying was directed at a student's weight, twenty percent contained sexist remarks, and eighteen percent was about perceived sexual orientation.

Some might think that bullying is nothing but harmless words or actions. That couldn't be further from the truth. Another recent survey reported that thirty percent of students who were bullied suffered from depression.[2] A surprising additional finding was that nineteen percent of those who bully others also suffered from depression. The American Foundation for Suicide Prevention reports that depression is a key risk factor for suicide and is the most untreated mental health disorder in youth.

Suicide resulting from bullying has now achieved its own term – bullycide.[3] Ac-cording to a study from the Yale School of Medicine, suicide rates are growing among adolescents and have increased by more than fifty percent in thirty years.[4] Some of the most publicized cases of bullying ended with the death of a young person. There is no doubt that bullying is a serious issue that can lead to tragic results.

So, why aren't people helping these young targets of bullying? Unfortunately, the answer is they likely don't know when specific incidents of bullying are happening. In 2011, the NEA reported that seventy-nine percent of bullying incidents go unre-ported.[5] It's difficult to help if no one knows a child is being victimized. However, teachers are in a good position to help with bullying situations because kids spend much of their time in school. The University of Michigan reports that kids spend thirty-two and a half hours per week in school, so educators can definitely make an impact.[6]

In order to address this bullying epidemic, however, parents, peers, and teachers have to be vigilant and proactive. A great way for adults to do this is by teaching social skills to young people. Learning specific social skills can help victims stand up for themselves and ask for help, bystanders recognize and report bullying, and bullies learn empathy. This book helps educators teach these skills in their classrooms.

The material here represents the collaborative effort of many individuals who have distinguished themselves in the fields of education, parent training, and family development. The authors and contributors combined the real issues regarding bullying with social skills and strategies developed by Boys Town's National Training program that have been successfully incorporated and used in public and private school systems throughout the country. Through these lesson plans, our experts share with you how to address skill deficits with the key players (bully, victim, and bystander), examine the impacts of bullying, and teach methods for problem solving.

The book is organized into three parts:

Part I   Understanding the Problem

Part II   Solving the Problem

Part III Appendix
(Tips for Educators and
Anti-Bullying Social Skills)

The content is focused on helping teachers determine what is needed and how to apply it best to the young people in need of skills. The book gives insight on the scope of the issue and various kinds of bullying, as well as ways to help solve issues related to bullying through teaching social skills and problem-solving methods.

The lesson plans can be used during class meetings, in proactive discussions, or at any time the educator feels is appropriate.

Nathan, Paige, and Emily are real-life accounts of the hardships and struggles bullying victims face. There are lesson plans with skills you can teach to help victims, including "Asking for Help," "Responding to Bullying," and "Making Friends." These skills can be lifesavers for kids like Nathan, Paige, and Emily.

For those who witness the pain experienced by victims, skills like "Showing Concern for Someone Who's been Hurt," "Reporting Other's Behaviors," and "Resisting Negative Peer Pressure" can give bystanders the courage to stand up to bullying behavior even if they are not directly involved.

And last but certainly not least, teaching the skills of "Accepting Differences," "Expressing Empathy and Understanding for Others," and "Apologizing," can help those who bully begin to change their own negative behaviors.

We hope this book serves as a valuable resource and tool for helping shape healthy adolescent relationships that are void of bullying. Let's strive to put an end to painful stories like those of Nathan, Paige, Emily, and countless other victims of bullying.

Footnotes

[1] Beware of the Cyber Bully. (n.d.). *i-SAFE America.* Retrieved January 11, 2011, from http://www.isafe.org/imgs/pdf/education/CyberBullying.pdf

[2] Harpaz, B. J. (2010). Bullying can be a red flag for depression. *msnbc.com.* Retrieved January 11, 2012, from http://www.msnbc.msn.com/id/36688350/ns/health-childrens_health/t/bullying-red-flag-depression/

[3] Bullycide - Bullying Statistics. (2009). *Bullying Statistics – Teen Violence, Anger, Bullying, Treatment Options.* Retrieved January 11, 2012, from http://www.bullyingstatistics.org/content/bullycide.html

[4] Ibid.

[5] Bradshaw, C. P., Waasdord, T. E., & O'Brennan, L. M. (2011). National Education Association's Nationwide Studying of Bullying. *www.nea.org.* Retrieved January 11, 2011, from http://www.nea.org/assets/img/content/Findings_from_NEAs_Nationwide_Study_of_Bullying.pdf

[6] U.S. children and teens spend more time on academics. (2004, November 17). *University of Michigan News Service.* Retrieved January 11, 2012, from http://www.ns.umich.edu/index.html?Releases/2004/Nov04/r111704a

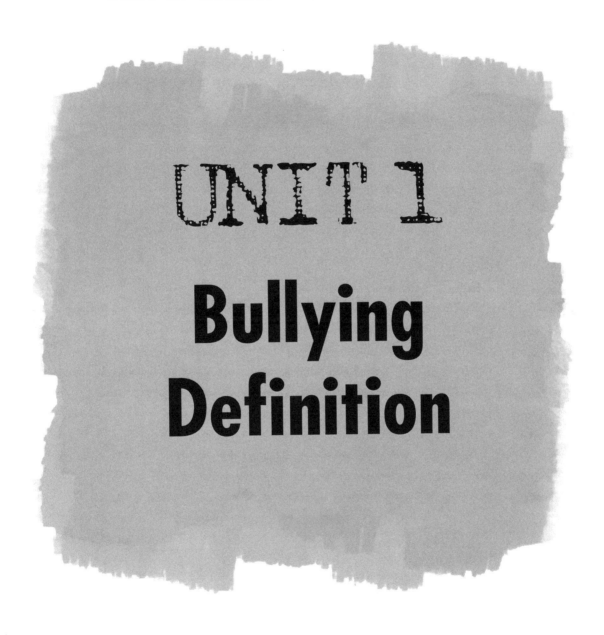

UNIT 1

Bullying Definition

LESSON 1 – **Identifying Bullying**

<table>
<tr>
<td rowspan="6">PART I UNDERSTANDING THE PROBLEM</td>
<td>OBJECTIVE</td>
<td>Students will be able to correctly identify instances of bullying.</td>
</tr>
<tr>
<td>MATERIALS</td>
<td>
• Pens/pencils
• "Is This Bullying ?" handout
</td>
</tr>
<tr>
<td>STEPS</td>
<td>
1. Give each student the handout, "Is This Bullying?," and allow them five minutes to complete it.

2. When five minutes are up, divide the students into five equal groups.

3. Assign each group one scenario from the handout and ask the group members to come to a consensus on their assigned scenario. Teacher records the groups' responses by scenario on whiteboard.

4. Have each group share whether their scene was bullying and explain why.

5. Teaching point/conclusion – emphasize to students the importance of paying attention to what is happening around them and to their classmates.
</td>
</tr>
<tr>
<td>OUTCOMES/ HOMEWORK/ FOLLOW UP</td>
<td>None</td>
</tr>
<tr>
<td>EXTENSIONS/ ALTERATIONS</td>
<td>None</td>
</tr>
</table>

Is This Bullying?

Nate is in the ninth grade and sits in front of Mia in math class. Mia kicks Nate's chair and whispers, "Don't you know the answer, Nate?"

    ☐ Bullying   ☐ Not Bullying

On your Facebook wall, your best friend posts "Hope you break a leg!" before opening night of the school play in which you are the lead.

    ☐ Bullying   ☐ Not Bullying

Emily, a new student, is in the cafeteria looking for a place to sit. At every table she passes, kids move closer together or say, "This space is saved." This has been going on since she came to the school a month ago.

    ☐ Bullying   ☐ Not Bullying

Tatiana's family is leaving on a ski trip. On her Facebook wall, Natalie posts, "I hope you break your leg." When Tatiana returns to school after the trip, her locker is plastered shut like a cast.

    ☐ Bullying   ☐ Not Bullying

A group of eight students are laughing in the hallway. Ethan says, "Zach, you are so fat! Did you swallow Jared from Subway?" All of the students laugh, including Zach who responds, "No, just his little brother." Everyone laughs more. Ella says, "Good thing you don't have a girlfriend, she couldn't even reach around you for a hug." The bell rings and Zach walks away from the group with a red face.

    ☐ Bullying   ☐ Not Bullying

LESSON 2 – **Fact or Fiction?**

PART I **UNDERSTANDING THE PROBLEM**	**OBJECTIVE**	Students will learn more about the facts of bullying.
	MATERIALS	• "Fact or Fiction Quiz" handout • Pens/pencils
	STEPS	1. Give each student the handout, "Fact or Fiction Quiz," and allow them five minutes to complete it. 2. When five minutes are up, have students partner up. 3. Tell the pairs to come to a consensus on each question. 4. Ask the various pairs to share their answer to a question with the class and explain why they chose that answer. 5. Review the correct answers and the reasons why with students.
	OUTCOMES/ HOMEWORK/ FOLLOW UP	None
	EXTENSIONS/ ALTERATIONS	None

Fact or Fiction Quiz

1. Bullies are mostly boys.   FACT or FICTION?

2. Large classes and big schools promote bullying.   FACT or FICTION?

3. Bullies usually don't have many friends.   FACT or FICTION?

4. Bullying is just a normal part of growing up.   FACT or FICTION?

5. Common bullying tactics girls use are
   manipulation, gossip, and exclusion.   FACT or FICTION?

6. The most common form of bullying among
   boys and girls is physical violence.   FACT or FICTION?

7. Bullycide is a term used to describe a suicide
   caused by bullying.   FACT or FICTION?

8. Most acts of bullying are never reported.   FACT or FICTION?

9. Bystanders who see bullying violence can be
   emotionally upset.   FACT or FICTION?

10. Bystanders are always afraid of the bully.   FACT or FICTION?

11. Once a bully, always a bully.   FACT or FICTION?

Fact or Fiction Quiz   ANSWERS

1. Bullies are mostly boys.   FACT or

Bullying defies gender. However, studies show some differences in how bullying is acted out by boys and girls. For example, males are more likely to engage in overt acts, such as punching, kicking, and posturing, while females report using more covert behaviors, such as gossip, rumor, and exclusion. Of course, these behaviors are never gender exclusive.

2. Large classes and big schools promote bullying.   FACT or FICTION?

Research suggests that there is no correlation between larger classes or schools and increased incidents of bullying. One Canadian study actually found that students in small schools bullied more. According to the researcher, the findings imply that victims of bullying in small schools may be "repeat victims" because it is more difficult for offenders to select different victims.

3. Bullies usually don't have many friends.   FACT or FICTION?

Research studies show that bullies often enjoy higher social prestige among their classmates. In one large-scale study, bullies indicated it was easier for them to make friends than it was for those who were victims.

4. Bullying is just a normal part of growing up.   FACT or FICTION?

Abusive relationships are not natural, nor should they ever be accepted as normal.

5. Common bullying tactics girls use are manipulation, gossip, and exclusion.    or FICTION?

Studies show that girls are more likely than boys to engage in covert behaviors that undermine relationships (gossiping, backstabbing, excluding, etc.).

6. The most common form of bullying among boys and girls is physical violence.   FACT or

Studies and research report that verbal bullying accounts for the majority of bullying behaviors, and that verbal bullying is starting at earlier ages.

7. Bullycide is a term used to describe a suicide caused by bullying.

Bullycide was coined by two authors who co-wrote a book by the same name. Suicide is the third leading cause of death for Americans between the ages of 15 and 24. While it's not known how many suicides result from bullying, experts believe it is often a contributing factor for adolescents. Risk factors for suicide include feelings of hopelessness and social isolation – two emotions that bullying victims know well.

8. Most acts of bullying are never reported.

Research suggests that bullying behaviors often go unreported for several reasons. Victims feel ashamed or are reluctant to tell out of fear the problem will escalate. Teachers and parents who react impulsively often end up compounding the problem as much as adults who choose to ignore it.

9. Bystanders who see bullying violence can be emotionally upset.

Bullying, whether it happens in a school cafeteria or a neighborhood pool, creates tension and anxiety in children. It has a detrimental effect on the entire social climate. At school, when children do not feel safe, they can't concentrate on learning. Instead, they focus on how to avoid being harassed as they walk to class, ride the bus, or walk home.

10. Bystanders are always afraid of the bully.

Some bystanders may fear the bully. Others simply don't know what to do, and still others worry they'll do the wrong thing if they intervene. Bystanders may make the situation worse by watching, laughing, and generally encouraging the bully's behavior.

11. Once a bully, always a bully.

No child is a lost cause. With patience, guidance, and instruction, children can be taught how to develop positive relationships with others and satisfy their needs by being assertive rather than aggressive.

PART I: UNDERSTANDING THE PROBLEM

UNIT 2
Key Players

LESSON 3 – **Bystanders**

OBJECTIVE		Students will understand their role as bystanders and how they can make a positive difference in the bullying cycle. (This lesson plan can be broken into several activities and used at different times.)
MATERIALS		• Handouts, sticky notes, or whiteboards for students • For art classes: drawing paper and markers • For computer classes: computer with color printer
STEPS		1. Skill to teach: Empathy 2. Ask students to define empathy (identifying with and understanding another's situation and feelings). 3. Divide class into groups of two. Have each pair come up with and write down a definition of empathy. 4. After two minutes, have the students write their answers on chart paper, whiteboard, etc. 5. Have the skill of and steps to "Expressing Empathy and Understanding for Others" written on a chart or board. The steps to the skill are: ❶ Listen closely to the other person's feelings or observe his or her actions. ❷ Express empathy by saying, "I understand…." ❸ Demonstrate concern through your words or actions. ❹ Offer assistance in a safe manner. Discuss how you might "tweak" this skill so it is more applicable to the class/group definitions of empathy. 6. **Background information for teacher, counselor, or leader to share with students** (do not share this research information until after the activity below):

PART I UNDERSTANDING THE PROBLEM

Research says that most bullying incidents (that are not "cyber" related) are witnessed by others eighty-eight percent of the time. A small percentage of the witnesses may be the bully's "henchmen" (the clique of friends or followers who accompany or help the bully). Most, however, are bystanders that include peers, teaching staff, or other adults like parents. Research also shows that when bystanders get involved the right way, more than fifty percent of bullying stops immediately. However, bystanders get involved less than five percent of the time.

There are many reasons why bystanders choose to stay outside or away from bullying situations, including:

- Some believe the situation is none of their business.
- Some believe the kid being bullied deserves it.
- Some think, "At least it's not me. If I interfere, I could be the next target."
- Some think that if they tell an adult, nothing will happen or they will be considered a tattletale or "narc."

With the help of the following activity, explore these and other reasons and give ideas to help students who are bystanders to safely get involved.

7. **Activity:**
   a. In small groups or with partners, have students answer the seven questions below. You can write them on the board or distribute the "Bullying and Bystanders" handout to the groups.
      - How often do you see bullying in school?
      - List at least one area where you see bullying take place often.
      - List two reasons why you think bystanders do not speak up or help a target of bullying.
      - Describe one incident where you saw someone step in or where you got involved in a bullying situation. What happened?
      - List one positive outcome you have experienced or witnessed in a bullying situation when someone got involved.

STEPS *(continued)*	• List one negative outcome you have experienced or witnessed in a bullying situation when no one got involved. • Describe a safe way to get involved in a bullying situation. b. Give ten to fifteen minutes. Everyone in the group should give an answer. c. Each group should have a recorder and a spokesperson. d. Have the groups' spokespersons share their answers with the class. If a group has the same answer as one being shared with the class, that spokesperson should raise his or her hand at the end of the answer.

**OUTCOMES/
HOMEWORK/
FOLLOW UP**
	1. **Good Samaritan Law Worksheet** – Have students read, talk about, and complete the worksheet to learn ways to safely tell an adult about a bullying incident. Also, role play safe ways for bystanders to tell.
	
	2. **Role plays:**
	   • **Situation 1:** Students are shooting hoops in the gym when a bully and his gang take the basketball from another student. You and two of your friends watch this happen. What do you do?
	   • **Situation 2:** A female student is in the bathroom trying to put in her contacts. A bully pushes the girl on purpose and she drops her contact on floor. What do you do?
	   • **Situation 3:** In the locker room, a bullying victim is pinned to a locker by a bully. What can you do?
	
	3. **Discussion Questions for the Good Samaritan Law Worksheet**
	   • How is being an involved bystander like the Good Samaritan Law?
	   • When you hear the term "Good Samaritan," what do you think of?
	   • How do you think this term can be related to bystanders (i.e., those who see bullying happening in their immediate area) in the bullying cycle?

OUTCOMES/ HOMEWORK/ FOLLOW UP (continued)	• Almost every state in the U.S. has a "Good Samaritan" law. Who do you think it protects? • Read the Good Samaritan Law description from the Good Samaritan Worksheet and write or discuss one of your thoughts on the Good Samaritan Law.
EXTENSIONS/ ALTERATIONS	1. **For Computer Classes:** Have students work in pairs to come up with anti-bullying slogan posters to place around school where students have indicated bullying takes place. Print the slogans on a color printer and laminate (if possible). Role play safe ways to get involved. 2. **For Art Classes:** Have an anti-bullying poster contest showing safe ways for bystanders to get involved. 3. **For Language Arts Classes:** In pairs, have students write a definition of empathy and why it is important in dealing with bullying. 4. **For Social Study or History Classes:** Ask these questions: • "Why do you think some countries during crises show empathy and others don't?" • "How do the ones that show empathy intervene?" Use examples involving natural disasters (e.g., tsunamis, earthquakes, etc.) wars (e.g., Iraq, Libya, etc.), or the latest news from television, radio, newspaper, or Internet.

Bullying and Bystanders

1. How often do you see bullying in school?

2. List at least one area where you see bullying take place often.

3. List two reasons why you think bystanders do not speak up or help a target of bullying.

4. Describe one incident where you saw someone step in or where you got involved in a bullying situation. What happened?

5. List one positive outcome you have experienced or witnessed in a bullying situation when someone got involved.

6. List one negative outcome you have experienced or witnessed in a bullying situation when no one got involved.

7. Describe a safe way to get involved in a bullying situation.

Good Samaritan Law

Good Samaritan Law

Good Samaritan Laws have been passed in many states to encourage people who see another person "in imminent and serious danger or peril" to go to that person's aid. The laws protect the rescuers from being sued for any damage that occurs from the rescue unless the assistance was "reckless or grossly negligent."

Answer the following questions:

1. If you saw a person (adult or child) obviously hurt or in need of assistance outside your school, would you help in some way?

    YES or NO

    If "Yes," how might you help? If "No," why? _____

    _____

    _____

2. Bullying comes in many forms and it hurts people. Only a small percentage of bystanders come to the victim's aid. Sometimes, bystanders may actually behave in ways that reinforce the bully's behaviors. What do you think the bystander behaviors below show? Be ready to explain your answer, either in your group, with your partner, or in class discussion.

    When you stand by and watch bullying behavior (physical, verbal, relational, or sexual) and do nothing, your presence is telling the bully or bullies it is okay.

    YES or NO

    When you laugh at what a bully is doing to a target or victim, you are telling the victim that you agree with the bully.

    YES or NO

When you laugh at what bullies are doing to targets or victims, you are telling the bullies to continue this type of behavior.

YES or NO

When you walk away and do nothing when bullies target victims, you are telling the victims you don't care about them.

YES or NO

When you react to bullies by using aggression (pushing or fighting back), you are stepping in in a safe way.

YES or NO

When you walk away and text a teacher or call a hotline number about a bullying incident, you are showing the character skill of caring.

YES or NO

When you tell targets to hang out with you, you are showing the character skill of courage.

YES or NO

When you tell the bully to "knock it off" and take the target with you, you are demonstrating the character skill of courage.

YES or NO

When you tell an adult to watch the hallway at school during a passing period because bullying is happening, you are trying to stop bullying in a safe way.

YES or NO

Complete one more "When you…" statement to challenge the group with.

When you _____

_____

_____

_____

LESSON 4 – **Bullies**

PART I UNDERSTANDING THE PROBLEM	**OBJECTIVE**	Students will understand that there are many actions to bullying and motivations behind why people bully.
	MATERIALS	• Whiteboard or SMART Board
	STEPS	1. Open a discussion about bullying and the profile of a bully today. Prompt the discussion by asking students to describe a typical bully. 2. In small groups or with partners, give students eight minutes to discuss the actions that bullies engage in and why a person might bully others. Have students prepare answers to add to the whiteboard/SMART Board. 3. When time is up, have one student from each group add the group's answer to the whiteboard/SMART Board. Ask students not to repeat a previous answer, only to add unlisted ones. 4. Follow with a discussion around the answers. Guide the discussion to the learning point that a bully is seeking power over targets in various ways and there is no typical profile of a bully. They come in different shapes, sizes, backgrounds, and genders.
	OUTCOMES/ HOMEWORK/ FOLLOW UP	As a follow-up, do Lesson 5.
	EXTENSIONS/ ALTERATIONS	This lesson can connect with/be followed by Lesson 5.

LESSON 5 – **Bullies**

<table>
<tr>
<td rowspan="9">PART I   UNDERSTANDING THE PROBLEM</td>
<td>OBJECTIVE</td>
<td>Students will further investigate why some people bully others.</td>
</tr>
<tr>
<td>MATERIALS</td>
<td>
• Paper
• Pens/pencils
</td>
</tr>
<tr>
<td>STEPS</td>
<td>

1. Optional: Review the information from Lesson 4.

2. Students are going to be investigators, looking for evidence as to why they think kids bully.

3. Divide the students into pairs.

4. Give five minutes for pairs to brainstorm and write down reasons why they think kids bully.

5. After five minutes, have one person in each pair stand up and move to the left or right so students now have new partners. The person who wrote the list takes it with him or her to the next pairing.

6. Give another five minutes for the new set of partners to continue brainstorming and adding reasons to their lists.

7. When time is up, have pairs choose the top three reasons from their lists to share with the class.

8. Have pairs either list or verbally share their reasons with the rest of the class. Facilitate a discussion around the reasons students share.

TEACHER NOTE: *Examples of reasons might include: They are mean. They are angry at someone else. They have been bullied by someone in their lives, like a brother, sister, or parent or step-parent at home. They are prejudiced. They don't like people who are different. They have not received care or love from appropriate people in their lives. They are seeking attention. They don't feel like they fit in at school. Their grades are bad and they deflect attention this way.*

</td>
</tr>
</table>

STEPS *(continued)*	9. Summarize the lesson by discussing that regardless of the reason, bullying others is not an appropriate or a healthy way to interact with others.
OUTCOMES/ HOMEWORK/ FOLLOW UP	Optional: As homework, ask students if they think bullies can change. If so, what steps could a bully take to change his or her behavior? Follow up by having students write a skill with the steps for "Stopping Bullying Behavior" and post the skills and steps around the room/school.
EXTENSIONS/ ALTERATIONS	None

LESSON 6 – **Victims/Targets**

<table>
<tr>
<td>**OBJECTIVE**</td>
<td>Students will gain skills for effectively dealing with bullying and safe ways to report it.</td>
</tr>
<tr>
<td>**MATERIALS**</td>
<td>
<ul>
<li>Paper for T-Charts or "Bullying and Bullying Targets" handout</li>
<li>"How to Handle Bullying: Yes or No" and "10 Ways to Safely Deal with Bullies" worksheets</li>
<li>Markers or pens</li>
</ul>
</td>
</tr>
<tr>
<td>**STEPS**</td>
<td>

1. **Unit introduction information for teacher, counselor, or leader:** High priorities for schools are safety and academic learning. However, research says that more than 160,000 students stay home from school daily because of bullying. If students aren't feeling safe and stay home, less academic learning takes place, and when they are at school, learning is more difficult due to an inability to concentrate.

2. **Group work:**
   - Divide class into groups/pairs.
   - Give groups eight minutes to discuss ways students have seen or heard targets handle bullying.
   - Ask each group to complete a T-Chart listing the bullying situation on the left, and how the bullying targets handled it on the right.
   - Have the groups/pairs present and discuss their T-Charts.
   - Debrief the students and make note when groups put down "fighting back" as a positive way to handle bullying. Discuss the similarities and differences of the charts to set up the follow-up worksheets.

</td>
</tr>
</table>

PART I UNDERSTANDING THE PROBLEM

OUTCOMES/ HOMEWORK/ FOLLOW UP	1. **Follow-Up Worksheet 1: How to Handle Bullying: Yes or No** This worksheet will help the groups or pairs of students consider how targets and victims of bullying can safely and more effectively deal with bullies. 2. **Follow-Up Worksheet 2: 10 Ways to Safely Deal with Bullies** This worksheet lists ten ways for victims/targets to safely deal with bullies and can be used in small discussion groups.
EXTENSIONS/ ALTERATIONS	None

Bullying and Bullying Targets

BULLYING SITUATION	HOW BULLYING TARGET HANDLED THE SITUATION

How to Handle Bullying: Yes or No

Circle "Yes" or "No" following each question. Be prepared to explain or defend your answer. You may begin by first answering the questions on your own, then share your answers with your partner or group.

1. You sit in the back of the room. One student always pokes you with a pencil or pen. The best way to deal with this is to turn around and yell, "Knock it off!"   YES or NO

2. You sit in the back of the room. Several students bug you when you try to work by making negative comments. You decide to send an email to the teacher that you would like your seat moved. This is a safe way to deal with the situation.   YES or NO

3. You get shoved into the lockers daily in the afternoon. You decide to fake being sick in the class before this happens so you can go home. This is a good way to deal with the situation.   YES or NO

4. You have been bullied by the same person for more than a year now and you finally tell your parents (or parent). They decide to call the bully's parents and yell at them. This is the best way to get this type of bullying to stop.   YES or NO

5. You receive a nasty text message from a bully who you know is having a slumber party. You save the text but don't reply to it. This is a safe way to handle the message.   YES or NO

6. You are threatened via a text message after school. So, the next day you bring an item that could be used as a weapon to defend yourself. This is a good way for you to stay safe.   YES or NO

7. A group of students makes fun of your clothes. You smile and say to them, "Thanks for noticing my creative style." This is a safe way of handling this situation.   YES or NO

8. You have been bullied physically, verbally, and emotionally. You decide to get a group together to be with you after school in order to physically confront the bullies. This is a good way to handle the situation.   YES or NO

Discuss your answers with your partner or group. For "No" answers, come up with better solutions.

10 Ways to Safely Deal with Bullies

Read these over and with your partner or group, circle the three you think are the best, safe ways to deal with bullies. Be prepared to discuss your selections with the class.

1. Tell a trusted adult at a safe time in a safe way as soon as possible. Avoid telling the adult when other students or siblings are around.

2. Walk away and ignore the present situation.

3. If you get angry, avoid talking, walk away, and try to calm yourself by using a calming strategy like counting to ten, deep breathing, etc.

NOTE

A victim/target needs to be aware of the surroundings and location in order to choose a strategy for dealing with a bullying situation safely.

4. Tell the bully to stop without using inappropriate language. Depending on the location, you might say, "I'd appreciate it if you would just leave me alone and stop the attitude." Or, you could say loudly, "Stop it. Leave me alone," and call the bully by name so someone hears it.

5. Walk with a group of friends or a friend and avoid non-safe areas whenever possible.

6. Avoid retaliation in the form of hurtful words, physical reactions, or cyber methods. (If you act like a bully, then you might be considered a bully, and the bully wins again.)

7. Use humor. For example, if a bully makes fun of your clothes, glasses, or something else you are wearing, you might say, "Thank you for your fashion advice." Or, you could simply say, "Thanks for noticing."

8. If bullying is continually happening at school, ask a parent or guardian to call or email your teacher. If things don't improve, have them call school administration. (Keep dates and records of all calls and emails.)

9. Avoid responding to bullying you get via email and text. However, keep them for proof. Check your school's policy on cyberbullying.

10. Be cautious when a bully or friends of a bully try to befriend you or ask you to dump a trusted friend. Never give a bully or friends of a bully any password information.

11. Try to expand your circle of friends by joining new groups or becoming active in a sport, club, or church group in or outside of school.

12. Celebrate You! Work on feeling good about yourself by doing things like standing tall, using an assertive voice, and listing your accomplishments.

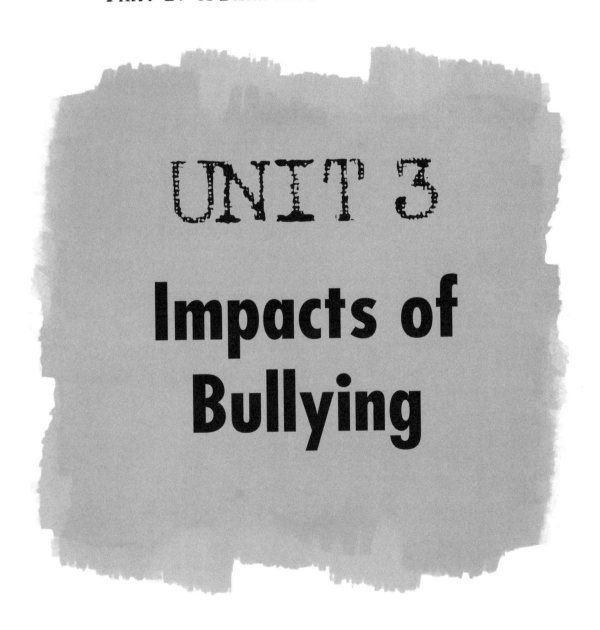

UNIT 3

Impacts of Bullying

LESSON 7 – **Bystanders**

PART I UNDERSTANDING THE PROBLEM	**OBJECTIVE**	Students will develop empathy for others.
	MATERIALS	• Slips of paper • Pens/pencils
	STEPS	1. Have students arrange their chairs in a large circle with the chair backs facing in. 2. Pass out slips of paper to each student and have them write down the meanest comment he or she could make to somebody (no swear words). 3. Collect slips of paper and mix them up. 4. Each student draws a slip of paper, takes a seat, and reads the comment aloud one right after another. 5. Students flip the paper over and write down how the comments made them feel (emotion) even though they were not directed at them. 6. Have the students talk about how the comments made them feel, how it would feel to have them all directed at them, and the importance of empathizing with others.
	OUTCOMES/ HOMEWORK/ FOLLOW UP	The outcome is to develop empathy in bystanders for others.
	EXTENSIONS/ ALTERATIONS	This activity is extended in the bully and victim lesson plans.

LESSON 8 – **Bullies**

PART I UNDERSTANDING THE PROBLEM	**OBJECTIVE**	Students will realize that one impact of bullying is a loss of friends.
	MATERIALS	None
	STEPS	1. This is a guided imagery exercise. Ask the students to close their eyes if they are comfortable doing so. 2. **Read this story:** You have a pet dog named Shaggy. When you come home, you go out back to play fetch with Shaggy. You throw the ball. He chases it, brings it back, and drops it at your feet. You say, "Good dog!" You turn to go inside and Shaggy barks at you. You pet his head and he nips at you, putting a hole in your favorite jeans. You say, "Bad dog" and he snarls and growls at you. This scares you a bit. You throw the ball again and Shaggy barks ferociously at you, which scares you enough that you go into the house. Later, Shaggy scratches at the door to come in. You let him in and he wags his tail and licks your hand as he passes by. While you are playing a video game, Shaggy starts chewing up one of your favorite shoes. You say, "Stop it!" and try to take the shoe away. Shaggy bares his teeth, growls, and will not let go of the shoe. Your shoe is ruined. While you are looking at it, Shaggy grabs your hand-held game and runs away with it. You finally get the game back, then go to your room and shut the door behind you so Shaggy cannot get in. 3. **Create a discussion around the following questions:** • What are your feelings towards Shaggy right now? (Possible response: "I wish Shaggy would go away.")

STEPS *(continued)*	• If Shaggy were a person and made you feel this way, would you want to be a friend? Why? (Students should say, "No, because he ruined my things, scared me, took things from me, and made me feel bad.") 4. **Teaching point/conclusion** – This is the impact of bullies and bullying. They hurt people and make others feel uncomfortable and scared. And, people don't want to be their friends. If you bully people, others will not want to be around you.
OUTCOMES/ HOMEWORK/ FOLLOW UP	This should decrease the perception that bullies are popular and have many friends.
EXTENSIONS/ ALTERATIONS	None

LESSON 9 – **Victims/Targets**

PART I UNDERSTANDING THE PROBLEM	**OBJECTIVE**	Students will realize the low self-esteem that can result from being a bullying victim.
	MATERIALS	• Slips of paper • Pens/pencils
	STEPS	1. Have students arrange their chairs in a large circle with the chair backs facing in. 2. Pass out slips of paper to the students and have them write down the meanest comment they could make to somebody (no swear words). 3. Collect slips of paper and mix them up. 4. Each student draws a slip of paper, takes a seat, and reads the comment silently, imagining that someone made that comment about or directed at them. 5. Students flip the paper over, write down how the comment made them feel (emotion), and draw an arrow up or down indicating if the comment improved or hurt how they feel about themselves. 6. Lead a discussion on the impact others' words have on how we feel about ourselves.
	OUTCOMES/ HOMEWORK/ FOLLOW UP	The outcome is to develop empathy for victims of bullying.
	EXTENSIONS/ ALTERATIONS	This activity is extended in the bully and bystander lesson plans.

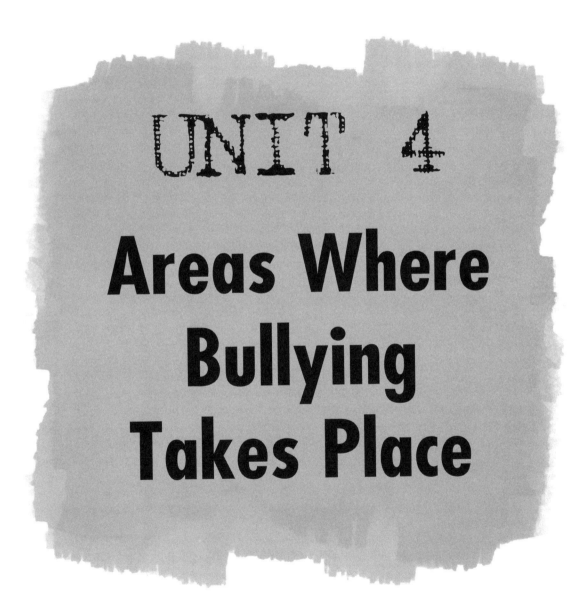

UNIT 4

Areas Where Bullying Takes Place

LESSON 10 – **Classroom Climate**

OBJECTIVE		Students will come to a consensus on what they want the classroom climate to be. Students will identify behaviors and commit to displaying those behaviors to maintain the classroom climate they decided on.
MATERIALS		• Chart paper/poster-sized paper • Markers
STEPS		1. Ask students what a "classroom climate" is. 2. Shape their answers to, "It is how the classroom feels." 3. Ask students to give words that describe how they want their classroom to feel and what kind of classroom climate they want. List their responses on the whiteboard/flipchart. (Possible answers: safe, respectful, positive, nice to each other, etc.) 4. Divide students into small groups/pairs. Have them make a list of behaviors that create the climate they described. (Possible answers: listen, wait your turn to talk, do your part, refrain from teasing/name-calling, etc.) 5. Give them three minutes to make their lists. 6. Have each group choose a spokesperson to share the group's list. Write the responses on the whiteboard/flipchart. Only add new behaviors to the chart as the groups share their lists. 7. If the list is more than ten, have the students vote on their "top ten." 8. Once the list is narrowed down, ask the students to commit to exhibiting these behaviors in order to create and maintain the positive, safe classroom climate they want.

PART I UNDERSTANDING THE PROBLEM

STEPS *(continued)*	9. Have a small group of students volunteer to create a poster for the classroom that displays the behaviors the class committed to. Then, have all students sign the poster to demonstrate their commitment to contributing to the classroom climate.
	10. Display the poster prominently in the classroom and refer to it throughout the year to remind and reinforce those behaviors.
OUTCOMES/ HOMEWORK/ FOLLOW UP	To follow up, refer to the poster and add to it if the students make suggestions.
EXTENSIONS/ ALTERATIONS	This same lesson could be done to create lists of behaviors to improve the climate for common areas, school grounds, and the school bus.

LESSON 11 – **Common Areas**

PART I UNDERSTANDING THE PROBLEM	**OBJECTIVE**	Students will be able to identify areas in the school that tend to be places where bullying takes place. Students will be able to identify where "safe zones" are located in the school.
	MATERIALS	• None needed – the activity will be a "field trip" around the school to identify at-risk areas and safe zones.
	STEPS	1. Once class has started and the hallways and other common areas are clear, take the class around the school – both inside and outside. 2. Highlight and discuss with students the areas that tend to have less adult supervision and the areas that tend to have more. 3. Discuss with them ways they can avoid areas where bullying tends to take place, and ways they can inform teachers of problem areas and bullying incidents.
	OUTCOMES/ HOMEWORK/ FOLLOW UP	• Continue a discussion with students regarding what areas in and around the school building feel the safest to them and those that carry a greater risk for bullying. • Ask students what they think could be done to make "unsafe" areas safer. • Empower students to "own" those areas. • Give students strategies to prevent and report bullying, such as intervening, getting help from an adult, and being assertive.
	EXTENSIONS/ ALTERATIONS	None

LESSON 12 – **School Bus**

<table>
<tr>
<td rowspan="5">PART I UNDERSTANDING THE PROBLEM</td>
<td>OBJECTIVE</td>
<td>Students will identify bullying behaviors that occur on the school bus and be able to offer appropriate actions to stop or report bullying.</td>
</tr>
<tr>
<td>MATERIALS</td>
<td>• Whiteboard/flipchart</td>
</tr>
<tr>
<td>STEPS</td>
<td>

1. Have students get in pairs.

2. Pairs have two minutes to brainstorm a list of bullying behaviors that occur on a school bus. Try to limit the list to only behaviors that take place on a bus. Remind students that bus rides include those to field trips and sporting events as well as to and from school.

3. After two minutes, have pair with the longest list write the list on the whiteboard/flipchart.

4. Go around to other groups and have them add any additional, different bullying behaviors they have on their lists.

5. Follow this with a discussion about each behavior and the appropriate action to take. For example, if the behavior is repeated (hard kicks to the seat) what should a bystander or the victim do? Ask the kicker to stop? Report the kicking to an adult (bus driver or monitor)? Should the person kick back? Facilitate a problem-solving discussion around each behavior to reach the most appropriate action/solution.

</td>
</tr>
<tr>
<td>OUTCOMES/ HOMEWORK/ FOLLOW UP</td>
<td>Ask students to try implementing an appropriate action next time they are on a school bus and encounter one of the bullying behaviors.</td>
</tr>
</table>

EXTENSIONS/ ALTERATIONS	If your students keep journals, have them write about an appropriate action they took or observed when they encountered a bullying situation.

LESSON 13 – **School Grounds**

OBJECTIVE		Students will be able to generalize appropriate behaviors inside the school building and outside the building on school grounds.
MATERIALS		• Paper • Pens or pencils
STEPS		1. On a piece of paper, have students identify appropriate behaviors that students should be expected to use in specific school grounds locations. (For example, in the student lounge, personal space should be respected by not standing too close to others when they are using the vending machines.) 2. Then ask the students to think of other areas of the school grounds where this expectation or behavior should be used as well. (Allowing people to have personal space should be respected also when working in small groups in the classroom or walking in the hallways. Or, students should move out of the way instead of running into someone on the playground.) 3. Have students share their responses and explain how they came to their conclusions/reasoning.
PART I UNDERSTANDING THE PROBLEM	**OUTCOMES/ HOMEWORK/ FOLLOW UP**	• Challenge students to transfer one expectation/action from one school grounds location to another during the week. • In the following weeks, have two students briefly share what expectation/action they transferred and how it worked for them. If they encountered any issue/problem, have the class problem solve future solutions.

EXTENSIONS/ ALTERATIONS	To extend this lesson, have students provide additional expectations/actions that should be set for various school ground locations to make them safer and to create "bully-free" zones.

LESSON 14 – **School Watch**

OBJECTIVE	Students will have a sense of ownership and community regarding behaviors that take place in the common areas in and around the school.	
MATERIALS	• Art supplies • Wall space • Writing/drawing utensils	
STEPS	1. Ask students to discuss what they can do to promote a safe school environment. 2. Have students create posters for the school hallways, parking lot, playground, or any other "un-owned" or unsupervised areas that promote these behaviors. 3. Have students include on their signs the consequences, impacts, and warnings regarding bullying behaviors. 4. Encourage students to "own" these areas by reporting bullying activity they see to appropriate school personnel.	
OUTCOMES/ HOMEWORK/ FOLLOW UP	Ask for student volunteers to "watch" these areas during the normal times in their day that they are in the problem common areas.	
EXTENSIONS/ ALTERATIONS	None	

(Sidebar: PART I UNDERSTANDING THE PROBLEM)

LESSON 15 – **Cyberbullying**

	OBJECTIVE	Students will understand the importance of keeping personal information private. Students will understand that when information is shared online or through text messaging, they lose control of how that information is used.
	MATERIALS	• Blank paper • Writing/drawing utensils • Classroom space
	ACTIVITY 1 STEPS	1. Have the students find their own private space in the classroom where they can feel alone. This helps to imitate the feeling of security they have at their home computer or on their cell phone. Talk with the students about how the personal space closest to them represents their privacy and that the open classroom space and all the students around them represent the Internet and its users. 2. Instruct students to write on their papers a bit of private information about themselves that they would only share with their very closest friends or family, and to write their name on the paper. Make sure the students know they must keep their eyes only on their paper. Students will then fold their papers in half. 3. The activity can proceed in one of two ways: • The teacher may say, "Now I would like you all to come up one at a time and give me your paper, starting with… (student's name). Once I have all your papers, I will read them to the rest of the class." • Or, the teacher may say, "When I give the direction to do so, I want you to give your paper to the person seated to your right so they can read what you have written."

PART I UNDERSTANDING THE PROBLEM

ACTIVITY 1 STEPS *(continued)*	4. **Do not read students' papers aloud or have them exchange papers. The point here is to make them understand how they feel when they believe their private thoughts are about to be shared.**
	
	5. Discuss with students the importance of guarding their privacy. Ask students what they felt when they thought their private information was about to be shared with the rest of the class. Prompt them to think about how the information they share with friends online or through text messaging can easily be sent to someone they don't want to share private information with.
	
	6. Inform the students that they should ask themselves the following questions before they post or text anything:
	
	   • "Is this information something I don't want other people to see?"
	   • "Will I be embarrassed if others see this information?"
	
	   If the answer to either question (or both) is "Yes," the information is private and they should not share it.
	
	7. At the end of the activity, instruct the students to tear or shred their papers into tiny pieces to ensure that none of the information inadvertently is shared with the class. The teacher is responsible for collecting and disposing of the pieces of paper.

ACTIVITY 2 STEPS	1. While at their desks, have the students create a drawing, a brief story, or a statement about themselves. Have them include their name on their paper. 2. Students will then pass their paper to another student (clockwise, counter-clockwise, or forward or backward). Next, instruct students to make changes to one another's work. Pre-teach that there should not be any changes that are malicious. Have the student's original work passed off to several other students and then eventually return each student's own work to him or her.

ACTIVITY 2 STEPS *(continued)*	3. Process with students the idea that once they hit the "send" button on an online post or digital message, they can never take it back. And, they cannot control what is done with the information once it is sent, including if someone decides to change it in a negative way. 4. Ask students to share what their original message or picture was and have them share what changes were made to it. Ask students how they felt when they saw the changes, and in knowing they had no control over what their peers might do to their original work. Highlight the importance of only sharing information with trusted family or friends, and that they need to think about how the information they share might be changed, manipulated, or distorted. Also, highlight that their intended audience may not be the only ones who gain access to the information, because information shared digitally is easily disseminated to potentially thousands of people with the click of a button. **TEACHER NOTE:** *With either activity, make sure students' original papers are ultimately returned to them. The goal in Activity 1 is not to actually share this information but to give the **impression** that it will be shared.*
OUTCOMES/ HOMEWORK/ FOLLOW UP	As a follow-up, do Lesson 16.
EXTENSIONS/ ALTERATIONS	None

LESSON 16 – **Cyberbullying**

	OBJECTIVE	Students will gain a better understanding of the impact negative comments have on others, as well as an understanding of how the anonymity of cyberspace emboldens many to say things they would not say to others face to face.
	MATERIALS	• Blank paper or whiteboard • Classroom space • Writing utensils
PART I UNDERSTANDING THE PROBLEM	**STEPS**	1. Introduce the activity by highlighting that bullying often occurs online, through the use of cell phones, and through other digital means. 2. Allow students time to write negative comments they have seen, heard, witnessed, or delivered themselves about others in text messages, on Facebook pages, etc. Have students write these on individual pieces of paper or on the whiteboard (one student at a time). 3. Pre-teach that they should not use the names of students who the comments were directed at or use comments that could identify individual students. 4. The teacher will then read aloud some of the comments or have students direct those comments at the teacher. This provides students the opportunity to see the effect negative comments have on victims. 5. Process and discuss with students how it felt to hear and see the reaction of the person they were directing their negative comments at. Ask students if they would actually say the things that were written down on the papers (or whiteboard) to another person face to face. Also, discuss ways students could put a stop to such

ACTIVITY 2 STEPS *(continued)*	such comments if they witness them online. Finally, remind students that posting comments via text messaging, Facebook, Formspring, Myspace, email, etc., leaves a trail back to the person who posts them.
OUTCOMES/ HOMEWORK/ FOLLOW UP	None
EXTENSIONS/ ALTERATIONS	None

UNIT 5
Special Topics

LESSON 17 – **Sexual Bullying**

	OBJECTIVE	Students will be able to identify, address, and problem solve "same gender" and "across gender" sexual bullying issues.
	MATERIALS	• Handout – "Sexual Bullying Scenarios" • Pens/pencils (optional) • Notepad (optional)
PART I UNDERSTANDING THE PROBLEM	**STEPS**	1. Place students into three equal groups. 2. Each student will receive a "Sexual Bullying Scenario" handout. (If these scenarios are not appropriate for your students, create new ones.) 3. Assign Scene 1 to Group 1, Scene 2 to Group 2, and Scene 3 to Group 3. 4. Have groups silently read their assigned scene. They have three minutes to do this. 5. Groups will discuss their assigned scenario together and determine how they would resolve the sexual bullying issue. 6. Have each group select a spokesperson. This person will share with the entire class how the group addressed and/or resolved their specific issue. **TEACHER NOTE:** *You may want to move around the room and monitor responses to this activity. Make sure that students' responses are thoughtfully developed. Solutions should not include retaliation or violence. Remind them that they should always talk to a trusting adult whenever they feel uncomfortable or violated.*
	OUTCOMES/ HOMEWORK/ FOLLOW UP	None

EXTENSIONS/ ALTERATIONS	Rather than selecting a spokesperson to "discuss" the group's answers to each scenario, students could "role play" the vignette, making sure to act out the appropriate solutions to each scene.

Sexual Bullying Scenarios

SCENE 1

Jeanette is the new girl at McLean Middle School. She moved to town one week ago and has no friends yet. Yesterday, while sitting alone at a cafeteria table, Mallory approached her and asked if she could eat lunch with her. Jeannette eagerly agreed.

Mallory stated that she noticed that Jeanette did not have friends at McLean, and said that she would become her friend if she allowed her to stroke her hair and touch her "beautiful long legs." Jeanette began to feel uncomfortable, but then realized she didn't want to lose a potential new friend. What should she do? How would you handle this situation?

SCENE 2

Monday morning, Mary entered her English class. Immediately, a group of girls began to stare her down and break into laughter as she sat down. Mary noticed that they were passing notes to each other. Every time Mary would glance over, the girls would look at Mary and continue to laugh.

As Mary left for her next class, Cynthia told her that the girls were spreading rumors about her. She said that Jonathan, Mary's next-door neighbor, told them that he and two other guys had sex with her over the weekend. Mary burst into tears. She screamed, "That's a lie! My grandmother was sick, so I spent the weekend at her house." How should Mary handle the vicious gossip?

SCENE 3

During an algebra exam, Trina pulled out a piece of paper from her purse. This paper contained answers to the test. James, another student sitting across from her, watched her every move. After Trina turned her paper in, James whispered in her ear, "If you don't give it up tonight, I'm going to tell Mr. Warren that I saw you cheating"! Trina broke out in a cold sweat. She wondered what to do because she was already failing her algebra class.

LESSON 18 – **Reporting Mechanism**

PART I UNDERSTANDING THE PROBLEM	**OBJECTIVE**	Students will brainstorm and learn a reporting process that empowers them to report acts of bullying to the appropriate adults.
	MATERIALS	• None needed – students may use paper and pen to take notes or create a flyer.
	STEPS	1. Facilitate a discussion with students about how, when, and in what ways they can report bullying acts that allow for discretion. 2. Teacher provides students with names and the availability of adults in the building who serve as authorities students can report bullying incidents to. 3. If desired, have students create a flyer with this information that they can pass out at a later time.
	OUTCOMES/ HOMEWORK/ FOLLOW UP	• Create flyer • Recruit teaching staff to aid in being available for student reporting.
	EXTENSIONS/ ALTERATIONS	None

LESSON 19 – **Trends in Bullying**

PART I UNDERSTANDING THE PROBLEM	**OBJECTIVE**	Students will identify and discuss current events and trends that are present in the media and/or culture of the school that deal with bullying.
	MATERIALS	• Newspaper, magazine, and online news articles/stories, as well as anecdotal evidence/experiences from students of bullying incidents at school.
	STEPS	1. The teacher and/or students will bring current news articles/stories to class for discussion. 2. Teacher talks with students about current trends in bullying, including various methods/means (e.g., Facebook, Formspring, email, text messaging, YouTube, etc.), "bullycide," acts of bullying that are filmed and posted on the Internet, sexting, etc. 3. Teacher can ask the students to share what events have occurred recently in their school that involve bullying. In this discussion, the teacher should help students identify the key players (bully, victim, bystanders) involved in the incident(s) as well as the best course of action for each player to take. 4. The goal of this lesson plan is to get students to think about and generate creative solutions to bullying incidents. Recent events will give students relevant and real-life context to do this.
	OUTCOMES/ HOMEWORK/ FOLLOW UP	None
	EXTENSIONS/ ALTERATIONS	None

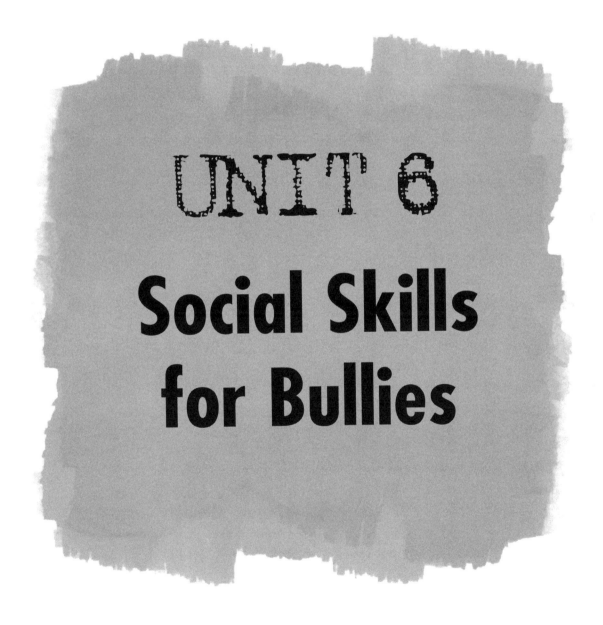

UNIT 6
Social Skills for Bullies

LESSON 20 – **Accepting Differences**

OBJECTIVE		Students will be able to recognize and learn that even though there are differences between themselves and others, there are also similarities. This can help students to appreciate and accept others' differences.
MATERIALS		• A small bowl of color-coated chocolate candies (such as M & Ms) and a small bowl of jelly beans • A picture of a cat and a picture of a dog • "Accepting Differences" skill poster (on CD) • Pens/pencils
STEPS		1. Break students into two groups. 2. Give one group the bowl of chocolate candies and the bowl of jelly beans. 3. Give the second group the picture of a cat and the picture of a dog. 4. Have both groups examine their items and brainstorm a list of **similarities** and **differences** between the two items they received. 5. Each group should select a "recorder" to write down all responses and a spokesperson to share the responses with the class. 6. After both groups have made their presentations, the teacher will display the steps to the skill of "Accepting Differences" to the class. (You can use the poster included on the CD or write them on your whiteboard.) ❶ Examine the similarities between you and the other person. ❷ Take note of the differences.

PART II SOLVING THE PROBLEM

STEPS *(continued)*	❸ Emphasize the shared interests, tastes, and activities between you and the other person. ❹ Express appreciation and respect for the other person as an individual. **TEACHER NOTE:** *This will provide an excellent opportunity for the students to make a connection between the initial activity and the social skill of "Accepting Differences."* 7. Explain each step to "Accepting Differences." 8. Ask students how each step and the skill as a whole can help decrease bullying instances.
OUTCOMES/ HOMEWORK/ FOLLOW UP	None
EXTENSIONS/ ALTERATIONS	None

LESSON 21 – Expressing Empathy and Understanding for Others

<table>
<tr>
<td rowspan="3" style="writing-mode: vertical">PART II   SOLVING THE PROBLEM</td>
<td>OBJECTIVE</td>
<td>To help students recognize that when they express empathy and understanding for others, it helps develop and strengthen relationships, and makes kids less likely to hurt or bully others.</td>
</tr>
<tr>
<td>MATERIALS</td>
<td>

• Handout: "Sanjay and Justin" story

• Handout: "How Empathetic Are You?" reflection sheet

• Skill poster (from CD)
</td>
</tr>
<tr>
<td>STEPS</td>
<td>

1. Ask students to think about a time when they were sad or upset.

2. Have them recall if anyone stopped to talk or show concern for them.

3. Ask students, "How did that make you feel?" (Allow for a three-minute discussion.)

4. Read the "Sanjay and Justin" story out loud to your students or hand out copies of the story and ask students to read it silently to themselves.

5. After you or the students have read the story, introduce the skill of "Expressing Empathy and Understanding to Others" to the class. Display and discuss each step and ask students to tell how each step relates to the story. (You can use the comments below as a reference.)

6. **"Expressing Empathy and Understanding for Others" Skill Steps:**

   ❶ **Listen closely to the other person's feelings.**
   With Sanjay and Justin, neither really listened. Justin replied to Sanjay's questions with questions about his own dad, and Sanjay didn't pick up on the fact that his friend was stressed out and didn't want to hear about weekend plans or science class.
</td>
</tr>
</table>

STEPS *(continued)*	**❷ Express empathy by saying something like, "I understand…."** Sanjay's way of telling Justin he understood his feelings was when Sanjay said, "That stinks," after Justin told him about not getting to see his dad very much. Sanjay's nonverbal behaviors (making more eye contact and really listening to his friend), especially after they argued, also showed empathy. Actions can communicate empathy as much as words can. **❸ Demonstrate concern through words and actions.** Sanjay showed his concern by apologizing for his behavior. He could see his friend was upset, and he felt bad that he pushed and yelled at Justin. **❹ Reflect back the other person's words by saying, "It seems like you are saying…."** Sanjay didn't use this step with Justin. You might not always do this step, especially when what you hear is so simple or clear that it's impossible to misunderstand what was said. Sometimes when it's obvious, repeating what was just said is awkward and unnecessary. However, if Sanjay had been confused by what Justin said or Sanjay wanted to make absolutely sure he understood, he could have said something like this: "I'd hate it if I didn't get to see my dad much. I guess that's why you're a little freaked out now, huh?" Remember though, if you're unsure or want to be absolutely positive you understand what someone said, just repeat what you heard using your own words. **❺ Offer any help or assistance you can.** Sanjay couldn't change the fact that Justin and his dad didn't see each other very much, and Sanjay couldn't make Justin's dad show up. But there was something Sanjay could do. He could keep his friend company until Justin's dad came – and that's what Sanjay did.

STEPS *(continued)*	7. Now, pass out the "How Empathetic Are You?" reflection sheet to students. Ask them to answer all questions honestly. Let them know no one will read their responses. The purpose of this activity is for students to self-reflect and determine if they need to become more empathetic and understanding to others.
OUTCOMES/ HOMEWORK/ FOLLOW UP	None
EXTENSIONS/ ALTERATIONS	None

Sanjay and Justin

I'm Sanjay, and I had a shouting match with my friend, Justin, because neither of us listened to the other. It happened on a Friday after school. I walked outside and saw Justin standing at the corner. He looked mad. He usually smiles a lot but this time he wasn't. He kept looking up and down the street like he was watching for someone.

I went over and asked him what was up. He told me he was waiting for his dad to pick him up, and that he should have been here by now. I shrugged and didn't think it was a big deal. I figured his dad was just late. That's when I started telling him about what I was going to do on Saturday.

I asked Justin what he was doing that weekend but he didn't say anything; instead, he asked me, "Why isn't my dad here yet?" I was like, "Geez, just chill out." Then I started telling him about a girl in my science class. I wasn't sure if he knew her so I asked him. He didn't say anything, so I figured that meant he knew her. I kept talking about how she broke two glass beakers in the lab.

While I was talking, he said something like, "Where is he?" And I said, "Where's who?" That's when he turned and looked at me and yelled, "My dad!" He was crying a little. I'd never seen him cry before. I asked him, "Dude, what's your problem?" Then he shoved me in the chest and yelled, "Haven't you been listening?" That made me mad so I shoved him back and yelled, "Were you listening to me?" It was wild.

I couldn't believe we got into a fight, and I didn't even know over what. Justin was crying even more. It sort of freaked me out. I felt bad and told him I didn't mean to be a jerk. Neither of us said anything for a while. Finally, Justin said everything was okay. He said he doesn't get to see his dad very much and he was scared and mad his dad had forgotten to pick him up.

I told him, "That stinks," and I said I would wait with him until his dad came. I didn't ask Justin why he never sees his dad but I did say Justin could come and hang out at my house if his dad didn't show up. Justin thanked me, and we both laughed a little. A few minutes later, his dad finally drove up.

"How Empathetic Are You?" Reflection Sheet

Directions: Circle one answer.

1. When others around you seem upset, does it affect your mood?
   - Always
   - Sometimes
   - Never

2. Do you ever get emotional when watching a violent or sad movie?
   - Always
   - Sometimes
   - Never

3. If a friend texted you and said he or she flunked a test, you would:
   - Reply right away with words of encouragement
   - Ignore the text
   - Reply with a "snarky" comment, like "sucks 2BU" or "awesome job"
   - Send a reply about something completely unrelated
   - Reply a day or two later

4. If you saw a homeless person under a bridge, your first thought would probably be:
   - Get a job, loser.
   - I hope he'll be okay.
   - Nothing. It doesn't bother me.

5. Do friends seek you out when they have problems?
   - Always
   - Sometimes
   - Never

LESSON 22 – **Making an Apology**

<table>
<tr>
<td rowspan="4" style="writing-mode: vertical">PART II SOLVING THE PROBLEM</td>
<td>OBJECTIVE</td>
<td>Students will learn the steps to the skill of "Making an Apology" and have the opportunity to critique public apologies according to the skill's criteria. Teacher will facilitate a discussion regarding how and why the skill should be applied to bullies and their behavior.</td>
</tr>
<tr>
<td>MATERIALS</td>
<td>

- Access to the Internet and video equipment and/or copies of newspaper and magazine articles.
- The skill steps of "Making an Apology" which are:
  1. Look at the person.
  2. Use a serious, sincere voice tone, but don't pout.
  3. Begin by saying, I wanted to apologize for…" or "I'm sorry for…."
  4. Do not make excuses or try to give reasons for your behavior.
  5. Sincerely say that you will try not to repeat the same behavior in the future.
  6. Offer to compensate or pay restitution.
  7. Thank the other person for listening.

</td>
</tr>
<tr>
<td>STEPS</td>
<td>

1. Ask students to consider and discuss answers to these questions:

   - "How do you feel about someone who makes a sincere apology?"
   - "How do you feel when someone uses excuses or tries to rationalize his or her behavior by saying things like, 'I did it because…' or 'This is your fault.'"
   - "What makes for a good apology?"
   - "What makes for a bad apology?"

</td>
</tr>
</table>

STEPS *(continued)*	2. Show students the skill steps of "Making an Apology" (skill poster on CD) and discuss them. 3. Use Internet articles, YouTube videos (politicians, celebrities, athletes, etc., apologizing for misstatements, slurs, or bad/embarrassing behavior), newspaper articles, magazines, websites, etc., for examples of apologies to critique. 4. Once students read about or view an apology, have them refer to the steps of "Making an Apology" and critique the person's apology based on the skill steps. 5. Allow students to share their interpretation of the apology. Facilitate a discussion about how and why bullies should apply the skill of "Making an Apology" to their own behavior.
OUTCOMES/ HOMEWORK/ FOLLOW UP	None
EXTENSIONS/ ALTERATIONS	• Write on the board the following quote from Voltaire: "No snowflake in an avalanche feels responsible." Have the students read the quote and think about how it ties into the steps of the "Making an Apology" skill. • Allow students time to discuss in small groups their interpretation of the quote based on the skill steps. Have groups share their thoughts with the class as a discussion point. End the lesson by revisiting the correct steps of "Making an Apology."

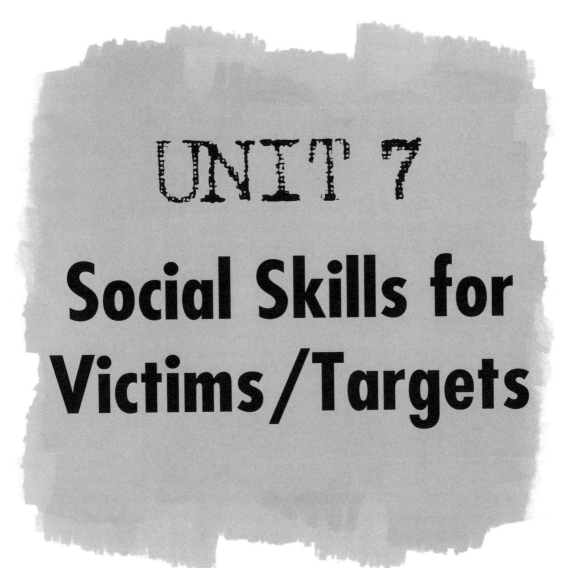

UNIT 7

Social Skills for Victims/Targets

LESSON 23 – **Making Friends**

PART II SOLVING THE PROBLEM	**OBJECTIVE**	To help victims learn to choose appropriate friends by looking for positive qualities/behaviors in a friend and the negative qualities/behaviors to avoid.

	MATERIALS	• "Friends" T-Chart handout
		
		• Handout with the skill steps of "Choosing Appropriate Friends, which are:
		  ❶ Think of the qualities and interests you might look for in a friend.
		  ❷ Look at the potential friends' strengths and weaknesses.
		  ❸ Match the characteristics of potential friends with activities and interests you share.
		  ❹ Avoid choosing friends who are unkind or involved with activities that are morally wrong or illegal.

	STEPS	1. Brainstorm with the class the qualities and specific behaviors to look for in a good friend and the qualities and behaviors to avoid. Put responses on a T-Chart, SMART Board, whiteboard, etc. **OR** 2. Break students into small groups and give each group the "Friends" T-Chart. Instruct them to come up with a list of qualities/behaviors to look for in a good friend and the qualities/behaviors to avoid. Give students five minutes. Then, discuss and share as a class. Have students post responses on a large T-Chart, SMART Board, whiteboard, etc. If another student has shared a similar quality/behavior, tell them to check it off their list and share a different one. 3. Discuss with class that even though they may know the desired qualities/behaviors and the ones to avoid when

STEPS *(continued)*	making friends, it still takes time and effort to develop healthy friendships. 4. Conclusion: Show the skill and steps of "Choosing Appropriate Friends" and explain how students have covered parts of the skill in their responses and discussion. Tell students you will post the skill and follow up at a later time.
OUTCOMES/ HOMEWORK/ FOLLOW UP	• In a future class, review the steps to "Choosing Appropriate Friends," discuss possible environments where kids can make new friends outside of your classroom, and talk about what steps they could take to make friends in these environments. • If students bring up making friends online, discuss the difficulties in assessing people's sincerity and truthfulness about themselves when there is no face-to-face interaction.
EXTENSIONS/ ALTERATIONS	None

Friends T-Chart

DESIRED QUALITIES/BEHAVIORS	QUALITIES/BEHAVIORS TO AVOID

LESSON 24 – **Asking for Help**

OBJECTIVE	Students will understand when and how to ask for help and why it is important for bullying victims to use the skill.	

MATERIALS	• Paper and pencils
	• The skill steps of "Asking for Help," which are:
	  ❶ Determine that you are in a situation you cannot resolve on your own.
	  ❷ Find a trusted peer or adult.
	  ❸ Let them know that you need assistance with an important matter.
	  ❹ Clearly describe the problem or what kind of help you need.
	  ❺ Thank the person for helping you.	

STEPS	1. Students will complete this activity individually. 2. Ask students to recall a situation in which they needed help and did not ask for it. (Particularly, a situation that turned out negatively because they didn't ask for help). 3. Use the handout on the CD to review the steps of "Asking for Help" with the students. 4. Have the students reflect/write a journal entry on their situation and how the skill would have helped create a better outcome. 5. Allow students who are willing to share their story and reflections of how the outcome would have been better or different if they had asked for help.	

PART II SOLVING THE PROBLEM

OUTCOMES/ HOMEWORK/ FOLLOW UP	Students will understand how and when to ask for help in response to bullying behavior. The goal is to help students to understand it is acceptable and important to seek help from others.
EXTENSIONS/ ALTERATIONS	None

LESSON 25 – **Teasing vs. Bullying**

OBJECTIVE		Students will identify and discuss the differences between teasing and bullying. The goal is to help students learn how to observe a situation and decide whether it is teasing or bullying. (Lesson 26 teaches students how targets can deal with bullying in an appropriate way.)
MATERIALS		• White board/chart paper • T-chart handout • Web chart handout
STEPS		1. Write this definition of "teasing" on the board: "Teasing is fun or horseplay between real friends." Underneath the definition, draw a T-chart with these headings: "Teasing" and "Bullying." Hand out copies of the T-chart worksheet to students. 2. Explain to students that sometimes kids and even adults will see or hear about a bullying situation and say it was "just teasing." This actually allows students and adults to condone bullying, and further damage can be done to the target of the bullying. The bullied student might even feel compelled to agree in front of the bully or bullies that he or she was "just being teased" and will laugh to cover up real feelings. 3. Ask students to think about and name the differences between genuine teasing and bullying. Write the differences on the T-chart under the appropriate headings. Some responses might be: Teasing creates stronger relationships; bullying damages relationships and is intended to harm the target. Teasing occurs between equals (age, intelligence, friendship); bullying occurs between people who are not equals in age, power (8th grader vs. 6th grader), etc. Teasing maintains

PART II SOLVING THE PROBLEM

STEPS *(continued)*	dignity of, respect toward person being teased; bullying is done to embarrass or hurt the feelings of the target. Teasing may include a harmless nickname that the target also thinks is funny; calling a target names that are derogatory or directed at his or her religion, ethnicity, speech, appearance, etc., is bullying.
	4. As you complete the T-chart, have students copy the differences onto their own T-charts.
	5. Draw a copy of the two Web charts in the handout on the board, one for the bully, the other for the target, and add these three headings on each chart: "Facial Expressions, Body Language, Voice Tone." Now ask students if they can describe some outward signs that someone is being bullied rather than teased.
	6. Pass out the handouts. As students suggest answers, write their responses on the board and have them fill in the web charts on their handouts.
	7. Look for answers like the following. Facial expressions: Target looks confused or hurt, won't make eye contact with the bully. Bully is smiling, smirking, or laughing in an unpleasant manner. Body language: Target is slumping or backing away. Bully is standing too close or aggressively moving toward the target. Voice tone: Target says nothing, responds very quietly or in a cracking voice. Bully is loud, sarcastic, laughing at, not with, target.
OUTCOMES / HOMEWORK / FOLLOW UP	Ask students to prepare for the next lesson by thinking about actual or fictional (TV, movie, book) bullying situations they have seen and how the targets responded.
EXTENSIONS / ALTERATIONS	None

Teasing vs. Bullying T-Chart

TEASING	BULLYING

Web Chart: Bully

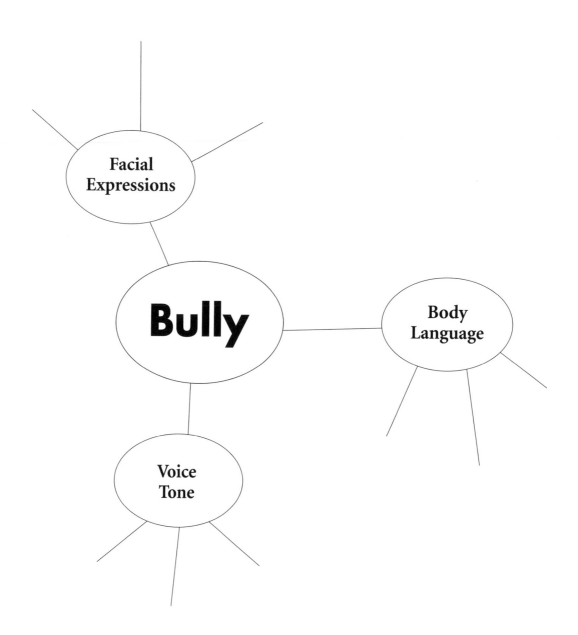

Web Chart: Target

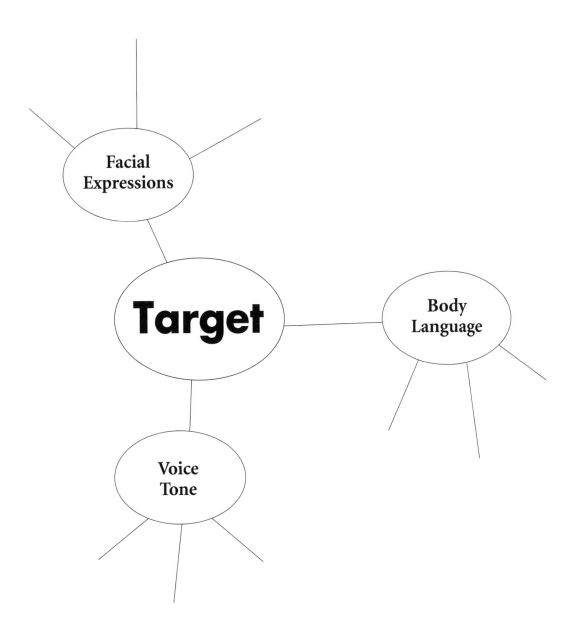

LESSON 26 – **Responding to Bullying**

OBJECTIVE		Teach students how targets of bullying can use the skill of "Responding to Bullying" in appropriate and safe ways.
MATERIALS		• Worksheet: "Put on Your Anti-Bullying Sunglasses" • Handout from CD with skill steps of "Responding to Bullying" which are: ❶ Remain calm, but serious. ❷ Assertively ask the person to stop the bullying behavior. ❸ If the behavior doesn't stop, ignore the other person or remove yourself from the situation. ❹ If the behavior stops, thank the other person for stopping. If appropriate and safe, explain how the behavior makes you feel. ❺ Report continued bullying or hazing to an adult.
STEPS	**PART II** SOLVING THE PROBLEM	1. Discuss with students that the purpose of sunglasses is to protect our eyes by filtering out harmful light. This "anti-bullying sunglasses" activity will help them filter harmless from harmful behavior. 2. Pass out the worksheet and give students a few minutes to consider and write an answer to the first instruction: Describe a bullying situation that you have seen personally, on TV, in a movie or book where the bully, bystanders, or adults claimed it was "just teasing." (Tell students not use a real situation if it involves or would embarrass anyone in the class.) 3. Direct students to answer the second question on the worksheet: What did you see or hear (facial expressions, body language, voice tone) that helped you decide that what was happening was bullying and not teasing?

STEPS *(continued)*	4. Write the steps to the "Responding to Bullying" skill on the board or use the handout from the CD. Go over the steps to the skill with your students. 5. Ask students to answer these questions on the worksheet: Did the target of the bullying handle it well? If not, how could the target use the skill of "Responding to Bullying" to do better in the future? 6. Have students consider the last question on the worksheet: What could any bystanders have done to help the situation? 7. Invite students to share the situations and outcomes of the bullying situations they witnessed.
OUTCOMES/ HOMEWORK/ FOLLOW UP	• Break the class into groups of three or four students each (or partners for smaller class sizes). • Ask groups to create a role-play, skit, or anecdotal presentation that describes or demonstrates a good response to one of the bullying situations.
EXTENSIONS/ ALTERATIONS	You can use a variation of this lesson plan in an English literature, history, or social studies class by asking students to answer questions on the worksheet while considering a bullying situation depicted in a short story, novel, or play the class is reading or an historic event they are studying.

Put on Your Anti-Bullying Sunglasses!

1. Describe a bullying situation that you have seen personally, on TV, in a movie or book where the bully, bystanders, or adults claimed it was "just teasing." (Do not use a situation involving any students in this class.)

2. What did you see or hear (facial expressions, body language, voice tone) that helped you decide that what was happening was bullying and not teasing?

3. Did the target of the bullying handle it well? If not, how could the target use the skill of "Responding to Bullying" to do better in the future?

4. What could any bystanders have done to help the situation?

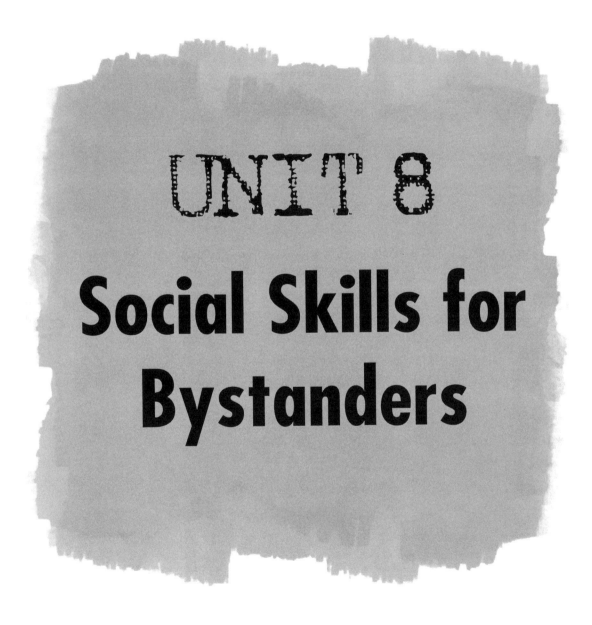

UNIT 8

Social Skills for Bystanders

LESSON 27 – **Resisting Negative Peer Pressure**

	OBJECTIVE	Teach students how to resist negative peer pressure.
	MATERIALS	• Handout on skill steps to "Resisting Peer Pressure," which are: ❶ Look at the person. ❷ Use a calm, assertive voice tone. ❸ State clearly that you do not want to engage in the inappropriate activity. ❹ Suggest an alternative activity. Give a reason. ❺ If the person persists, continue to say "No." ❻ If the person will not accept your "No" answer, ask him or her to leave or remove yourself from the situation. • "Bullying Places and Situations" rating sheet
PART II SOLVING THE PROBLEM	**STEPS**	1. Ask students to share with an elbow partner what resisting negative peer pressure means to them. Give two minutes. Ask for volunteers to share. 2. Next, use the skill poster handout from the CD or write the skill steps to "Resisting Peer Pressure" on a paper chart, SMART Board, whiteboard, etc. Have students discuss each skill step with their elbow partner, including what steps they could use more often or better, what steps they might change some of the words for, and what the meaning of each step is. Give three minutes. Ask for volunteers to share. 3. Finally, pass out a bullying rating sheet to each student and ask them individually (and without putting their names on the paper) to rank on a scale from 1-10 (with 1 being the least difficult up to 10 being the most

STEPS *(continued)*	difficult) how hard it is for them to resist negative peer pressure in the following places or situations: • In class • In restrooms • In commons area • During lunch • In hallways during breaks • On playground • After school • At parties • On the computer • At school activities (athletic events, school dances) • Other _____ 4. Give three minutes for students to finish this rating activity. Then ask students to share their thoughts about places where it's hardest and easiest to avoid negative peer pressure. Is there anything students could do to make it easier to deal with peer pressure in the places and situations that were rated the most difficult?
OUTCOMES/ HOMEWORK/ FOLLOW UP	None
EXTENSIONS/ ALTERATIONS	None

Bullying Places and Situations

On a scale of 1 to 10, rate how hard or easy it is to resist negative peer pressure when you are in these places. Use 1 for the easiest places to avoid peer pressure up to 10 for the hardest or most difficult peer pressure situations you face.

	EASIEST								HARDEST	
In class	1	2	3	4	5	6	7	8	9	10
In restrooms	1	2	3	4	5	6	7	8	9	10
In commons area	1	2	3	4	5	6	7	8	9	10
During lunch	1	2	3	4	5	6	7	8	9	10
In hallways during breaks	1	2	3	4	5	6	7	8	9	10
On playground	1	2	3	4	5	6	7	8	9	10
After school	1	2	3	4	5	6	7	8	9	10
At parties	1	2	3	4	5	6	7	8	9	10
On the computer	1	2	3	4	5	6	7	8	9	10
At school activities (athletic events, school dances)	1	2	3	4	5	6	7	8	9	10
Other _____	1	2	3	4	5	6	7	8	9	10

LESSON 28 – **Reporting Others' Behavior**

	OBJECTIVE	Students will learn to identify the difference between tattling and reporting the behavior of others. Also, they will develop strategies to report dangerous behavior. Finally, students will demonstrate the skill of "Reporting Others' Behavior."
	MATERIALS	• Skill sheet handouts (from the CD) with the steps of "Reporting Others' Behavior," which are: ❶ Find the appropriate adult or authority figure. ❷ Look at the person. ❸ Use a clear, concerned voice tone. ❹ State specifically the inappropriate behavior you are reporting. ❺ Give a reason for the report that shows concern for your peer. ❻ Truthfully answer any questions you are asked.

PART II SOLVING THE PROBLEM	**STEPS**	1. Hand out the skill steps of "Reporting Others' Behavior" to the class.
		
		2. Ask students to define or explain the difference between tattling and reporting. "Tattling is something you do to get someone into trouble. Reporting is something you do to keep someone safe or protected."
		
		3. Read each of the following scenarios to the class. Ask students to raise a hand if they believe it would be tattling if they …
		   • reported to a teacher that a peer ripped a poster in the hallway.
		   • reported to a teacher that a peer posted a nude picture on Facebook.

STEPS *(continued)*	• reported to a teacher that a peer cut in on a lunch line. • reported to a teacher that a peer brought a weapon to school. 4. Lead a discussion on what kinds of bullying behaviors need to be reported to keep victims or targets safe. 5. Ask students if they ever failed or hesitated to report dangerous behavior for fear of being called "a snitch." Discuss how finding a confidential way to report such behavior could avoid this. 6. Review and discuss the steps of "Reporting Others' Behavior." 7. Instruct students to make an action plan for how to report bullying behavior to an adult, and then have them write a description or outline of the plan in their journals.
OUTCOMES/ HOMEWORK/ FOLLOW UP	Student should be able to see the difference between tattling and reporting. Student also will have an action plan of how to report behavior confidentially.
EXTENSIONS/ ALTERATIONS	Have students brainstorm a bullying situation they should report to an adult. Have them journal the benefits of writing an anonymous report about the bullying behavior to a teacher instead of reporting verbally.

LESSON 29 – **Showing Concern for Someone Who's Been Hurt**

OBJECTIVE	Students will learn how to show compassion and concern for individuals who have been hurt or affected by bullying behavior.	
MATERIALS	• Paper for students to write on • Pens/pencils	
STEPS	1. Pass out blank sheets of paper to students.	
	2. Direct students to write what they would do in three sentences or less to each of the following three questions. Stress that the students can't write more than three sentences. Tell them not to put their names on the paper.	
	3. **Question 1:** "What would you do if you walked by a person your age who was crying?" (Allow one to three minutes for writing.)	
	4. **Question 2:** "What would you do if you heard a peer yelling hateful things to another peer?" (Allow one to three minutes for writing.)	
	5. **Question 3:** "How do you feel when someone says or does something mean to you?" (Allow one to three minutes for writing.)	
	6. Instruct students to fold their papers and exchange them five different times. That means the papers will be passed around to five people and when students receive a paper the fifth time, they stop, open, and read it.	
	7. Ask students to think back to what they wrote. Ask if they see any common patterns in what they wrote to what they just read. (Did others offer to help? Did others feel sad, angry, or hurt?)	

PART II SOLVING THE PROBLEM

STEPS *(continued)*	8. Collect papers from students. (Tear up and discard them later.)
	
	9. Discuss the skill steps of "Showing Concern for Someone Who's Been Hurt":
	
	  ❶ Calmly talk to the victim privately or ask him or her to join you and your friends.
	
	  ❷ Express concern by saying something like, "I saw what they did (or said) to you. It's mean and you don't deserve to be treated like that."
	
	  ❸ Invite the person into some positive activities with you and your friends.
	
	  ❹ Find common interests and positive things to share and say to the person.

OUTCOMES/ HOMEWORK/ FOLLOW UP	None
EXTENSIONS/ ALTERATIONS	None

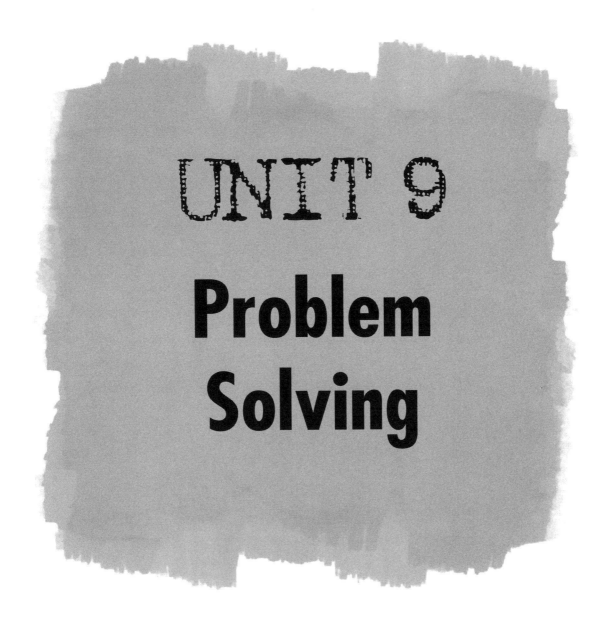

UNIT 9

Problem Solving

LESSON 30 – **POP – Problem, Options, Plan**

	OBJECTIVE	The learner will be able to apply the POP method to solve a problem.
	MATERIALS	• POP worksheets to hand out
PART II SOLVING THE PROBLEM	**STEPS**	1. Have students work in pairs to generate a list of problems/issues at the school. Give them two minutes to write down as many ideas as they can.
		2. Write on the whiteboard/flip chart each pair's "Top Two" problems/issues from their lists.
		3. As a class, identify one problem that everyone can use for the POP problem-solving method.
		4. Using the POP worksheet, have each pair identify several options on how to solve the problem and then decide on a plan to implement one of the options.
		5. Ask one group to share their POP worksheet with the class.
		6. Ask if any other groups came up with the same/similar plan. Generate a discussion around how groups determined their options and the thought processes used to reach their plan.
		7. Ask for another pair to share a different plan and repeat the previous discussion format.
		8. Summarize the activity by highlighting the differences in thought or reasoning and how these impact why people solve problems differently.
	OUTCOMES/ HOMEWORK/ FOLLOW UP	• Optional homework: Assign each pair of students a problem from the list until each team has two (or one if that's all the list allows) problems/issues to work on.

OUTCOMES/ HOMEWORK/ FOLLOW UP *(continued)*	A problem/issue can be assigned to more than one pair. • Have students follow the POP method to solve the problem. • If it's a problem with a plan that can be carried out, have them try to solve the problem and write a short summary of how it went. • Schedule a time to follow up on these assignments in two weeks. • Facilitate a discussion to debrief and explore the application of the POP process.
EXTENSIONS/ ALTERATIONS	POP can easily be used in academic lessons – e.g., use POP to solve a problem faced by a character in literature, to come up with a solution to a scientific or math problem, etc.

Problem Solving with POP

P = **Problem**
Identify the problem situation.

O = **Options**
List several possible options to solve the problem.

P = **Plan**
Formulate a plan to solve the problem based on one or more of the options.

LESSON 31 – **Problem Solving with SODAS**

OBJECTIVE		The learner will have a clear understanding of the SODAS process (Situation, Options, Disadvantages, Advantages, Solution) for problem solving.
MATERIALS		• Chart paper and markers OR separate whiteboards/ SMART Boards • SODAS worksheet • Optional: Cans or bottles of sugar-free soda to reinforce the students for their work
STEPS		1. Divide the students into five equal groups. 2. Assign each group one of the five letters to SODAS. Using the SODAS worksheet, cut it into five pieces with each letter at the top and give each group a letter. 3. Each group has ten minutes to come up with a way to teach their letter's step in the problem-solving process. 4. Monitor the groups as they work, keeping them on task and providing guidance when needed. 5. Each group teaches the other groups their letter's step in the problem-solving process. Have them present in order: "S" goes first, "O" second, "D" third, "A" fourth, and "S" last. 6. Close activity by giving each student a soda to reinforce their work, and summarize the SODAS process by giving examples of its application. **Example:** You (the student) walk through the commons area when you see a female classmate, who appears upset, surrounded by five or six older students. They have her surrounded and are laughing, pushing, and not letting her leave.

PART II SOLVING THE PROBLEM

STEPS *(continued)*	S – The **situation** is a classmate being bullied by older students. O – **Options** are to ignore the situation, report it to a teacher/counselor/principal, or try to stop the situation. D – A **disadvantage** of ignoring the situation is the classmate may get hurt physically or emotionally and the older students will likely continue to bully others. A **disadvantage** of reporting to an adult is that the older students (bullies) may find out that you reported the bullying. A **disadvantage** of trying to stop the situation is that you may get bullied or hurt as well. A – An **advantage** to ignoring the situation is that no one will know you saw it and there will be no time lost for you. An **advantage** to reporting the bullying is the behavior stops and your classmate is helped to be safe and secure. An **advantage** to trying to stop the bullying is that you may stop it and/or make a friend of the victim. S – After weighing the advantages and disadvantages, the best **solution** is to report the bullying to help keep the classmate safe and stop it from happening to others by this group of older students.
OUTCOMES/ HOMEWORK/ FOLLOW UP	• During the next week, have students apply the SODAS process to a problem and make notes regarding how it worked. Have students present at least one situation with the class that they feel comfortable sharing. • A week later, revisit SODAS and ask for students to share how they applied the process. • If a solution didn't work as well as expected, have students go over the options, disadvantages, and advantages again and come up with a different or modified solution to try.
EXTENSIONS/ ALTERATIONS	You can blend the SODAS process into academics by having students write in their journals, write papers, create play scripts, discuss theories, etc., about topics in various subjects.

Problem Solving with SODAS

S = **Situation**

Describe what the situation is, who is involved, when it happened, and where it happened.

O = **Options**

Brainstorm all the possible options to address the situation.

D = **Disadvantages**

List possible disadvantages to EACH option.

A = Advantages

List possible advantages to EACH option.

S = Solution

Consider the advantages and disadvantages to the options, and then select an option as a solution to try.

LESSON 32 – **Class Meetings**

OBJECTIVE		The learner will identify the guidelines for class meetings and understand the purpose for them.
MATERIALS		• Whiteboard/flipchart paper and markers
STEPS		1. Ask students why they think class meetings are conducted. (Expected responses include: to solve problems, communicate, and discuss areas of concern such as bullying).
		2. Post four flipchart papers/divide the whiteboard into four sections with one of the following headings on each page: Self, Peers, Adults, Property.
		3. Ask students to individually brainstorm ways to show or demonstrate respect to self, peers, adults, and property during a class meeting. Give students thirty seconds to make their lists.
		4. Have students take two minutes to write their responses on the whiteboard in the respective four sections. If it's how to show respect to oneself, it goes in the "Self" area; if it's showing respect to other students, it goes in the "Peers" area; etc. An item can be listed in more than one area.
		5. Once the lists are complete, divide the class into four groups and give each group one of the areas: Self, Peers, Adults, and Property.
		6. Have each group create one or two guidelines/rules for class meetings based on their assigned area and list. Give five minutes for this.
		7. Have groups present their guidelines/rules and have the rest of the class agree or disagree whether they should be added to the class meeting guidelines list.

PART II SOLVING THE PROBLEM

STEPS *(continued)*	8. Once guidelines are agreed upon, review with the class and ask students how these rules will help class meetings when trying to solve problems. (Expected responses include: "If we show respect to everyone, we can work together to come up with the best solutions to issues.")
	9. Summarize by posting the guidelines and schedule the next class meeting.
OUTCOMES/ HOMEWORK/ FOLLOW UP	• As homework, have students provide one issue for the class meeting agenda. The guidelines will be leveraged to solve problems.
	• With student input on how frequently they think they need or want to address school or classroom issues, schedule class meetings one time each week, month, or quarter. Also let students know that class meetings can be called at any time to discuss urgent issues.
EXTENSIONS/ ALTERATIONS	None

LESSON 33 – **Reporting Guidelines**

PART II SOLVING THE PROBLEM	**OBJECTIVE**	The learner will understand the guidelines for reporting behavior and demonstrate application of the guidelines.
	MATERIALS	• School's/district's reporting guidelines • Scenarios handout
	STEPS	1. Distribute copies of the school's/district's reporting guidelines. If none exist, speak with your administration. 2. Ask students to read them over and clarify to ensure students understand each guideline. 3. Divide students into pairs and hand out bullying scenarios copied from the CD. 4. Have pairs read the scenarios and apply the reporting guidelines to determine what actions to take. 5. Facilitate a discussion around each scenario and coach the students' responses to guide them to apply the reporting guidelines correctly and take appropriate action. 6. Summarize by answering any questions and reviewing the follow up.
	OUTCOMES/ HOMEWORK/ FOLLOW UP	Have students apply the guidelines outside the classroom to ensure behavior that should be reported is being reported. During the next class meeting or in a couple of weeks, ask students if they have any questions about the guidelines. Avoid asking about any specific reporting of events.
	EXTENSIONS/ ALTERATIONS	None

Reporting Guidelines Scenarios

1. Walking down the hall, you notice a student standing at his locker. Two older students walk over to him, push him against his locker, and put an arm against his chest. The younger student looks nervous as one of the older students says something to him harshly. The younger student digs into his pocket and hands the older student money. The older student removes his arm from the younger student's chest, hits him in the face with a light slap, laughs, and walks away.

   WHAT DO YOU DO? _____

2. Walking into the common area, you hear a girl say in a weak, almost crying voice tone, "Please don't!" You look over and see a girl trying to grab a cell phone as three other girls are laughing; one of them is texting on the phone. The girl who is texting says to the girl trying to grab the phone, "What's your problem? I'm just letting everyone know what a lesbo you are. Come out of the closet already!" The three girls walk away, laughing. The one girl is left behind trying to control her crying, while looking around to see who heard or saw what happened.

   WHAT DO YOU DO? _____

3. Walking into class, you hear one classmate say to another, "You're such a slut. I'll be following you home tonight to get some of what you're giving to everyone else."

    WHAT DO YOU DO?

4. Two boys are sitting in the cafeteria eating the lunches they brought from home. A group of four other boys are sitting next to them. As you watch, the four boys laugh, take food from the other two boys, and throw it on the floor, stepping on some. The two boys look down and don't say or do anything. The four boys leave, laughing.

    WHAT DO YOU DO?

5. While checking Facebook, you see postings about a classmate that you think are nasty and hurtful. The postings include: "You are such a freak."

    "How can you live in that ugly, fat body. Get lipo!"

    "You're a loser! Seriously, just jump off a bridge and end your misery. Or, do you need a push?"

    "FAG!"

    WHAT DO YOU DO?

PART III: APPENDIX

Tips for Teachers

1. Be observant – not only in your classroom but also in the "un-owned" areas of the school such as hallways and stairwells that don't always have direct adult supervision.

2. Model positive behavior in your nonverbal and verbal communication.

3. Teach social skills proactively and empathetically.

4. Teach social skills as replacement skills to negative behaviors, and do so in a calm manner.

5. If you supervise an area other than your classroom, be on time to that area and interact with students, not other adults.

6. Respond to bullying individually with the perceived bully, bystander, and victim. Do not respond to all three at the same time.

7. Keep track of all emails, phone calls, meetings, and reports from parents, administrators, and students that have to do with bullying incidents in some type of log, electronic folder, or other tracking means.

8. Keep administrators up to date in accordance with your school policy. If you are unclear of the policy, ask for clarification from your administrative team.

9. Keep a log of your positive phone calls, emails, and other correspondence with parents and students whenever possible.

10. Involve your students in solving problems through class meetings and problem-solving methods like SODAS, POP, and suggestion boxes.

11. Celebrate the positives with students!

Tips for Administrators

1. Pick some classes to survey* about bullying at the school to get a good sampling, then examine the results. This will give you baseline data to work from for future planning. Administer the same survey later in the year to the same groups.

2. Create a policy against bullying for your handbook that includes cyberbullying. (Zero tolerance is not recommended by researchers because it does not solve the problem.)

3. Have consequences in place for bullying that are based on intensity, frequency, and duration. Brainstorm consequences with your team. Keep records of incidents in the students' referral logs or create bullying logs. Have students write up an incident, sign the incident report, and date it. The administrator who handled the incident should also sign the report. Be aware that bullying incidents require investigation and that consequences may sometimes not be vetted immediately. Make this bullying report process part of your school handbook.

4. Evaluate the "un-owned" areas in the school for bullying incidents. These areas can include the commons area, cafeteria, hallways, stairwells, bathrooms, gym, playground, parking lot, etc. Have student council members and the leadership team be part of this evaluation. This helps focus your supervision on the various areas and allows you to better explain to the supervisors of those areas what to expect.

5. Give staff an in-service training and follow up on any bullying issues based on your data. Invite parents and board members to these trainings.

6. Devise safe and anonymous ways for bullying to be reported.

7. Reinforce students and staff for their efforts in dealing with bullying.

8. Avoid discussing a bullying incident with both the perceived victim and the perceived bully at the same time.

9. Avoid conflict resolution for bullying. Most research indicates it does not work.

10. Make sure all staff – and not just the counselors, deans, etc. – teach to and address bullying incidents and issues when they take place.

11. Celebrate with staff and students the efforts to reduce and eliminate bullying.

12. Form a committee for ongoing support of bullying prevention.

*Several examples of surveys are included in "No Room for Bullies" (2005, Boys Town Press)

Tips for Teachers Working with Parents about Bullying Incidents

1. Understand most parents have unconditional love for their child, whether he or she is a bully, victim, or bystander. Many times, it is difficult for parents to see and understand the whole picture.

2. Be confidential. Do not tell parents what other parents said or what other students did or said. Do not give out names of the students involved; parents will find that information out on their own. Respect the privacy of others, just as you would with a medical issue.

3. Stay calm and empathetic. Let parents know that the incident is an ongoing investigation and that you will stay alert and aware. Keep your conversations with parents as brief and positive as possible.

4. When you talk to a concerned parent, take notes and date each entry. Keep the records so you have them for possible use in the future.

5. Avoid discussing any bullying situations in the teacher's lounge or with other teachers unless they are part of your investigation, and then do so in a private area.

6. Keep your administration involved and notified of all developments.

7. If you hold a conference with an angry parent, ask an administrator or counselor to be present and involved.

8. Become more observant of all student participants who are involved in an incident.

9. Let parents know you will continue to reinforce and teach the appropriate social skills ("Getting Along with Others," "Showing Respect to Others," etc.) to bullies, bystanders, and victims. Encourage parents to do the same at home.

10. Make positive phone calls to parents whenever possible. Record, date, and log the interaction.

11. Share with parents the Boys Town Hotline number (800-448-3000) and give them a Boys Town Hotline card (if available) so they know where to go for support and assistance. Also, share with them Boys Town's parenting website (www.parenting.org) and the Boys Town teen website (www.yourlifeyourvoice.org).

Anti-Bullying Social Skills

Note: Black-and-white and color posters of these skills are included on the CD.

Skills for Bullies

Accepting Differences

❶ Examine the similarities between you and the other person.

❷ Take note of the differences.

❸ Emphasize the shared interests, tastes, and activities between you and the other person.

❹ Express appreciation and respect for the other person as an individual.

Expressing Empathy and Understanding for Others

❶ Listen closely to the other person's feelings.

❷ Express empathy by saying something like, "I understand…."

❸ Demonstrate concern through words and actions.

❹ Reflect back the other person's words by saying, "It seems like you are saying…."

❺ Offer any help you can.

Making an Apology

❶ Look at the person.

❷ Use a serious, sincere voice tone, but don't pout.

❸ Begin by saying, "I want to apologize for…" or "I'm sorry for…."

❹ Do not make excuses or try to give reasons for your behavior.

❺ Sincerely say that you will try not to repeat the same behavior in the future.

❻ Offer to compensate or pay restitution.

❼ Thank the other person for listening.

Skills for Victims

Choosing Appropriate Friends

❶ Think of the qualities and interests you might look for in a friend.

❷ Look at the potential friends' strengths and weaknesses.

❸ Match the characteristics of potential friends with activities and interests you share.

❹ Avoid choosing friends who are unkind or involved with activities that are morally wrong or illegal.

Asking for Help

❶ Determine that you are in a situation you cannot resolve on your own.

❷ Find a trusted peer or adult.

❸ Let them know that you need assistance with an important matter.

❹ Clearly describe the problem or what kind of help you need.

❺ Thank the person for helping you.

Responding to Bullying

❶ Remain calm, but serious.

❷ Assertively ask the person to stop the bullying behavior.

❸ If the behavior doesn't stop, ignore the other person or remove yourself from the situation.

❹ If the behavior stops, thank the other person for stopping. If appropriate and safe, explain how the behavior makes you feel.

❺ Report continued bullying or hazing to an adult.

Skills for Bystanders

Resisting Peer Pressure

❶ Look at the person.

❷ Use a calm, assertive voice tone.

❸ State clearly that you do not want to engage in the inappropriate activity.

❹ Suggest an alternative activity. Give a reason.

❺ If the person persists, continue to say "No."

❻ If the person will not accept your "No" answer, ask him or her to leave or remove yourself from the situation.

Reporting Others' Behavior

❶ Find the appropriate adult or authority figure.

❷ Look at the person.

❸ Use a clear, concerned voice tone.

❹ State specifically the inappropriate behavior you are reporting.

❺ Give a reason for the report that shows concern for your peer.

❻ Truthfully answer any questions you are asked.

Showing Concern for Someone Who's Been Hurt

❶ Calmly talk to the victim privately or ask him or her to join you and your friends.

❷ Express concern by saying something like, "I saw what they did (or said) to you. It's mean and you don't deserve to be treated like that."

❸ Invite the person into some positive activities with you and your friends.

❹ Find common interests and positive things to share and say to the person.